# Multilingualism

## Also available from Continuum

*Children's Language and Multilingualism*, Edited by Jane Simpson and Gillian Wigglesworth

*Multilingualism: A Critical Perspective*, Adrian Blackledge and Angela Creese

*Multilingualism, Citizenship and Identity*, Julie Byrd Clark

## Other Books by John Edwards:

*Challenges in the Social Life of Language*

*The Irish Language*

*Language and Disadvantage*

*Language and Identity*

*Language Diversity in the Classroom*

*Language in Canada*

*Language, Society and Identity*

*Linguistic Minorities, Policies and Pluralism*

*Minority Languages and Group Identity*

*Multilingualism*

*The Social Psychology of Reading*

*Un mundo de lenguas*

# Multilingualism

## Understanding
## Linguistic Diversity

### JOHN EDWARDS

continuum

**Continuum International Publishing Group**

The Tower Building
11 York Road
London
SE1 7NX

80 Maiden Lane
Suite 704
New York
NY 10038

**www.continuumbooks.com**

**British Library Cataloguing-in-Publication Data**
A catalogue record for this book is available from the British Library.

ISBN: HB: 978-1-4411-2348-0
PB: 978-1-4411-2695-5

**Library of Congress Cataloging-in-Publication Data**
A catalog record for this book is available from the Library of Congress.

Typeset by Deanta Global Publishing Services, Chennai, India
Printed and bound in India

*For Mike and Marnie, with love and appreciation*

# CONTENTS

# PROLOGUE

On 11 May 2011, as I was preparing the final draft of this book, former American president Bill Clinton came to speak at my university. The occasion was the opening of a new centre, established to encourage leadership in matters of public policy, business and health. President Clinton did not mention language, but he made several remarks about group affiliation, noting in particular the need to 'overcome identity differences'. Identity, he suggested, ought not to be defined in terms of what you reject in others but, rather, should rest upon a more intrinsic sense of self and self-direction. We need not always agree with others, but we might spend more time considering what we hold in common; we should move beyond respect for diversity to its celebration. These identity matters, Clinton argued, undergirded all attempts at renewed leadership and development in the modern world. In its demonstration – sometimes implicitly, sometimes directly – that language is a central component in group identity and its negotiation, this book underscores the president's timely observations.

First published in somewhat different form, in Catalan and Spanish editions, this book can only touch upon many important topics that are covered more thoroughly elsewhere – many of them in earlier works of my own, a number of which I have immodestly noted in the end matter. It does, however, present an overview of multilingualism that is reasonably complete, if abbreviated, and I hope that it will prove interesting and informative for a general readership. It may also serve as a supplementary text in language and linguistics courses. Following the final chapter, I have provided some referential guidance; however, in the interests of reading fluency and 'user-friendliness', I have omitted reference markers in the body of the text.

A short book requires only a short introduction. My intention in writing this one has been twofold. First, I wanted to present a picture of global linguistic diversity, with some of its important ramifications and consequences. Second, I wanted to point out that the most compelling aspects of this diversity are not linguistic at all – they have to do, rather, with the symbolic and identity-marking features of language. If languages were only instruments of communication, there would still be a great deal to say in a world that contains several thousand of them: why there are so many, how different they are from one another, how they present reality in different ways to their speakers and so on. It would also be useful, particularly for speakers of big languages, to discuss in some detail the multilingual capacities that characterize the majority of the world's population, the normality of multilingualism and the statistically minor category of monolingualism.[1]

But there is a great deal *more* to say when we realize that languages are totems as well as tools. For then we enter the highly charged psychological and social domains of group attachments, the most powerful and the most historically interesting categories here being ethnic and national affiliations. Even a cursory glance at the table of contents of this book will reveal my attempts to comment upon the intertwining of language and group identity.

I set the scene in Chapters 1 and 2 (The Diversity of Languages and Interpreting Language Diversity) by touching upon some of the early debates about the 'first' or the 'original' language, by pointing out that there are no 'primitive' or undeveloped varieties and by discussing the difficulties in ascertaining just how many languages there are in the world. There are

---

[1] When discussing languages and language groups, I have not put words like 'small', 'big' and 'large' in the inverted commas that they really require – this, simply to avoid tedious over-use. Readers will realize, of course, that the terms refer to the relative scope and dominance of languages. I am saying nothing about the size of speech communities nor, more importantly, am I making any sort of value judgement.

still many linguistic regions that remain poorly understood, and there are problems with the categorization and naming of dialects and languages. In Chapter 3 (Multilingual Abilities), I consider the extent of multilingualism around the globe. One of the central themes here is the ubiquity of multilingual capabilities and the relative rarity – except, perhaps, within the anglophone world – of monolingualism. At the same time, it is important to realize that, for most people, a bilingual or multilingual repertoire is an instrumental response to mundane needs. A corollary is that speakers' different fluencies are generally quite varied in their depth and extent. Chapter 4 (The Emergence and Measurement of Multilingualism) continues this part of the story by discussing the circumstances in which multilingualism typically arises and the difficulties that often emerge when we try to assess its extent among individuals and societies.

Chapters 5 and 6 deal with the ramifications of multilingualism. Just as extended language repertoires usually come about in response to real necessity, so are there obvious and frequent requirements to transcend language boundaries. In Chapter 5 (The Consequences of Babel: Lingua Francas), I discuss the use of bridging varieties. These fall into three categories: existing 'natural' languages that have risen to prominence because of the socio-political clout of their users; linguistically simple or restricted varieties – pidgin and creole languages; and 'artificial' languages, purposely constructed by their makers to be simple, regular and easy to learn. In Chapter 6 (The Consequences of Babel: Translation), I turn to the most immediate bridge across linguistic divides: translation. This has always been an intriguing quantity, despite its obvious merits and the need that it so clearly fills. On the one hand, inadequate translations interfere with the smooth and accurate transition from one language to the next; on the other, fluent translation has historically been regarded as a potential quisling, with the potential to carry details of group narratives, the stories and myths that we tell about ourselves, to other ears. The contemporary complaint of 'voice appropriation' is relevant here. I also discuss the very real difficulties inherent in translation exercises *per se*, suggesting that every act of translation also involves interpretation and judgement.

If language in its symbolic and identity-bearing role is important to the group, it follows that attempts will be made to protect it and to keep it 'pure'. Just as translation may carry secrets across group lines, so were linguistic influences coming the other way often seen as foreign contaminants. Thus, in Chapter 7 (Keeping Languages Pure), I discuss purism and prescriptivism. Under these headings, we observe the efforts to maintain languages in some mythical pristine state, efforts that are generally doomed to fail because of their political and linguistic naïveté, but efforts that are nonetheless of great psychological and social interest. While linguists themselves have traditionally shied away from prescriptive interference in the life of language, leaving the field to amateurs of various stripes, some contemporary scholars, motivated largely by the plight of the world's small languages, have argued for active intervention. I also point out in this chapter that – putting aside linguistic activism undertaken for nationalistic and group-identity purposes – some degree of prescriptive standardization became necessary with the advent of printing and literacy. The obvious requirements here account for the rise of language academies and councils around the world, as well as the codifying efforts represented in the work of lexicographers.

Languages and their cultures are dynamic, not static, entities. As circumstances change over time, it is natural to expect development and alteration. They are, as well, constantly in touch with neighbouring varieties: they will influence some and be influenced by others. In Chapter 8 (Languages and Identities in Transition), I pay attention to these processes. What are the important features bearing upon shifts in language usage, upon the maintenance of some varieties and the decline of others? Again, I stress here the importance of language-as-symbol. If languages were solely instrumental in nature, it is unlikely that we would see the emergence of such highly charged language-contact settings. Accepting that they are much more than mere tools, however, makes it easy to understand the lengths to which people will go in such settings. Chapter 9 (Endangered Languages and the will to Survive) follows up the discussion of language dynamics with a return to some of the prescriptive and protective emphases outlined in Chapter 7. I consider here the motivation behind language-revival efforts and try to make two central points. First, the history of such efforts shows very clearly how difficult (one might really say impossible) it is to attempt any sort of revival in isolation from the very social factors that have created the language crisis itself. Second, the importance of sufficient collective *will* can hardly be over-estimated, and so I give some considerable attention to this matter.

In the final chapter (Linguistic Intervention, and the 'New' Ecology of Language), I continue with the theme of support for flagging languages: why is it seen as so important, and how have scholars responded to the situation of endangered varieties? The most recent manifestations of concern here are found under the heading of the 'ecology of language', an endeavour that styles itself the modern, 'green' perspective on understanding language contact and conflict. I try to show here that, in fact, it is a very restricted sort of ecology – one essentially motivated by the desire for the preservation of linguistic diversity and the protection of small languages. There is, of course, nothing at all wrong with such a stance, but I argue that it is disingenuous to present it under the broad heading of 'ecology'. My discussion in this chapter is also meant to illustrate some of the internal flaws and errors in this 'new' ecology.

Finally, a short Epilogue draws together the main themes of this book. Overall, I hope that the treatment provided here will prove useful for readers seeking an introduction to an area that is of perennial interest and concern, an area that is of particular relevance at times – like our own – of social change and political negotiation, an area that reflects and highlights a very powerful intersection of factual information and social passion.

John Edwards
Nova Scotia, June 2011

# CHAPTER ONE

# The Diversity of Languages

## The First Language

In the story of Babel, the divine punishment for human temerity was the confusion of languages. But, if linguistic diversity first occurred at this point, what was the original language, the divine variety? For a very long time, this was a question of greatest importance, and it generally took the form of enquiry into the language of Eden. After all, *Genesis* tells us that after God had made all the birds and beasts, he 'brought them unto Adam to see what he would call them: and whatsoever Adam called every living creature, that was the name thereof'. Once, then, there was an original and ideal language and, unlike all languages since, there was a mystical but perfect correspondence between words and the things that they named. The early speculations here are, of course, without linguistic or historical merit, but they are of considerable psychological and social interest because they reveal what an important contribution language has always made to our sense of who we are. And what could be more important than being able to show that your language was, in fact, the very first one (or, at least, a lineal descendant of that 'Adamic' variety)? The implications for group and individual identity, for relations with other people and for communication – both instrumental and symbolic – are great. The 'winner' here would be able to claim both linguistic and cultural superiority. The search for the divine language, then, is the earliest example of something that remains of considerable importance in all discussions of multilingual contact and conflict, because these almost always involve bigger and smaller varieties of greater or lesser social force, languages with which speakers have very close affiliations and about which they hold very strong opinions.

Debate about the first language persisted for a long time. Even though Thomas Hobbes pointed out in the seventeenth century that there was no scriptural evidence for any particular language and even though (as he added) Adam's language was in any event lost at the tower of Babel, enquiries were carried out throughout the eighteenth century. The general opinion was that Hebrew was the original language, but many others were also suggested, including the Celtic languages, Flemish, Danish, Swedish, Polish, Basque, Hungarian, Breton, German and Chinese. Claims for these languages were not unrelated, of course, to political developments and aspirations. Some assertions were both pointed and amusing. One seventeenth-century writer argued that God spoke Spanish to Adam, the Devil spoke Italian and Adam and Eve subsequently apologized to God in French. Some Persian scholars felt that Adam and Eve spoke their language, the snake spoke Arabic and Gabriel spoke Turkish. Even at the time, of course, there were many who saw how ludicrous things were becoming: one satirist suggested that God spoke Swedish, Adam spoke Danish and Eve was seduced by a snake that spoke to her in French.

Another early approach to finding linguistic primacy in a multilingual world involved experiments with infants. Herodotus reports that the Egyptian pharaoh, Psamtik, arranged for two babies to be nurtured without hearing any language. At the age of two, the infants apparently said *becos*, a Phrygian word meaning bread. Early in the thirteenth century, the Holy Roman Emperor attempted a similar experiment, but without success, for it was found that 'the children could not live without clappings of the hands, and gestures, and gladness of countenance, and blandishments'. Later on, James IV of Scotland put two infants with a dumb woman, and 'some say they spoke good Hebrew'. All of these attempts were based on the assumption that, if left uninfluenced, children would somehow come out with the original language. This rather bizarre idea went unsupported, of course, not least by the naturally occurring 'experiments' provided throughout history by 'wolf-children' and 'bear-children'. None of these feral youngsters were able to speak, and most efforts to teach them a language were failures. Victor, the 'wild boy of Aveyron', discovered in 1799 aged about 11, is the best known case here.

Putting these ill-considered speculations aside, the question of language origins remains a puzzle. Was there one original language (the principle of *monogenesis*) or did several emerge more or less simultaneously, in different places (*polygenesis*)? And, in either case, just *how* did language arise? We are obviously on shaky ground here, so much so that, in 1866, the Linguistic Society of Paris forbade all further discussions on language origins, on the grounds that all would be fruitless. Only relatively recently has the question been given renewed attention. Modern ideas of language origins are embedded in an evolutionary picture in which the development of speech had survival value. A very recent theory, one that is of some particular relevance to group solidarity, holds that the utility of language was originally linked to social bonding. Gossip, the banal exchange of social experiences, is seen as a sort of human 'mutual grooming'. The most proficient speakers might have improved their survival chances by being more informed and more manipulative. The theory is controversial, but the universality of gossip – which accounts for about 70 per cent of everyday talk – is indisputable.

## Comparing Languages

However, wherever and whenever human language first arose, the scholarly community is virtually as one in the assertion that all known varieties are of considerable complexity: there are no 'primitive' languages, none is more 'logical' than any other, no 'exotic language' full of sounds unfamiliar to the western ear should be thought to signal any inherent neurocognitive variation between the inhabitants of Amazonia and those of Arizona. It is easy to point to differences – sometimes very striking differences indeed – across languages, and history reveals many instances in which particular variations have been seized upon to make one sort of case or another. Language A has no words for numbers higher than ten. Speakers of language B have a colour lexicon that makes no distinction between green and blue. The vocabulary of language C reveals its speakers' belief that stones have a vital life force. Would we be right to assume that the first group is mathematically illiterate, that the optical rods and cones of second-group members are deficient, and that the third-community animists are mired in dark-age ignorance? Possibly, although further reflection might show that the complex kinship vocabulary of the first group shows a refinement and nuance far exceeding that found in any 'developed' language, that the desert-dwelling members of the second community have separate words for dozens of subtle shades of brown – rivalled in western societies only by the usage of paint manufacturers and interior decorators – and that those benighted animists have a system of tenses that puts even classical Greek verbal complexity to shame.

The point here is a simple one: languages develop according to the needs of their speakers. There are no 'primitive' forms, but, equally, there are few languages that are ' over-developed'. Why have a higher-order number system if there is no necessity to go beyond something like 'one, two, three, many'? Why bother with many shades of green and blue when you live in the Sahara? And what, in a pre-scientific society that – like all societies – finds it necessary to understand its surroundings, could be more reasonable than to explain the mysteries of nature in essentially spiritual terms when no other explanations are available? A final point here: we can be certain (because we have any amount of evidence) that if the living conditions of members of groups A, B and C change, their languages will change, too, in accordance with altered circumstances. Those desert-dwellers will soon fine-tune their blue-green spectrum once they've struck oil and moved to the south of England.

Words themselves are only indicators. The real meaning of scholarly assertions about linguistic adequacy is that language keeps pace with conceptual advancement, which in turn determines the very needs of which even speakers can be aware. While there must obviously be a finite lag between new ideas and new terms, this lag varies inversely with the general importance of the idea. How long did it take for 'astronaut' to enter common usage? And, even while it was waiting to make its entrance, there were all sorts of other descriptive terms to fill the temporary void ('spaceman'). Description, albeit rough, is always possible.

Languages are best seen as different systems reflecting different varieties of the human condition. Although they may be unequal in complexity at given points, this does not imply that some have greater overall expressive power. To put it another way, we could say that not all varieties have the same capabilities: different social, geographical and other circumstances determine what elements will be needed and, therefore, developed. All are, however, potentially functionally equivalent. Languages differ in lexical, grammatical, phonological and other ways, but questions of overall linguistic 'goodness' are simply wrong-headed.

Different languages interpret and codify the world in different ways, and a moment's reflection will surely lead to the conclusion that the great variation in physical and social environments, over time and space, would make any other arrangement nonsensical. To repeat, however, no language has been found which is inadequate for the current needs of its users. To the surprise of some, acceptance of this idea has quite a long history. In the sixteenth century, for instance, Joachim du Bellay pointed out that 'all languages are of a like value ... to each man his language can competently communicate every doctrine', and he went on to reject the idea that 'diverse tongues are fitted to signify diverse conceptions'. Historically, this may have been a minority view, but it is now the received scholarly wisdom. The famous linguist, Edward Sapir, thus observed in 1921 that

> the lowliest South African Bushman speaks in the
> forms of a rich symbolic system that is in
> essence perfectly comparable to the speech of
> the cultivated Frenchman ... When it comes to linguistic
> form, Plato walks with the Macedonian swineherd,
> Confucius with the head-hunting savage of Assam.

Sapir's phrasing here is no longer quite *comme il faut*, perhaps – and there is more head-hunting now in corporate jungles than in those of Assam – but his words are endorsed by all linguists. That this endorsement is not shared by everyone outside the academic cloisters is one of the many reasons why a broader and deeper general awareness of language and languages is always to be encouraged.

## Languages and Language Families

How many languages are there in the world? Which are the most widespread, and which ones have the greatest number of speakers? It turns out that these are not easy questions to answer. In the early twentieth century, the *Académie française* identified some 2,800 different languages, and German scholars argued for about 3,000. A British estimate, however, suggested that there were 1,500 languages in the world. Contemporary scholars suggest a much higher figure: perhaps 4,500 languages. This is variability of a large order, and it obviously reflects a lack of sufficient linguistic knowledge.

The world may be much smaller now than it once was, but there are still areas that remain little known. In parts of Africa, South America and Oceania, for example, the linguistic jigsaw still lacks some pieces, while having others that don't seem to fit. Consider the island of New Guinea, for instance: it is perhaps the richest and most complex linguistic area in the world, and is home to many groups and languages about which we know very little. It is the second largest island in the world (after Greenland) – almost a continent in itself, in fact, although geologically Australian. The history of human habitation is exceptionally long: almost 60,000 years. New Guinea is home to many ecosystems, ranging from mountains to savannas to rain forests; consequently, the range of biodiversity is immense. There is equal breadth of human cultural and linguistic diversity: among a population that may be as high as eight million, there are perhaps 1,000 language communities. The size of the island, its challenging terrain, and its complicated and often troubled history have all contributed to make our knowledge far from precise. In some areas, indeed, we are faced with Rumsfeldian 'known unknowns': we are aware that there remain dozens of communities still designated as 'uncontacted tribal groups', particularly in the western half of the island (which is part of Indonesia).

Languages are arranged in *families* of related varieties, about which our knowledge is relatively recent. In 1786, Sir William Jones presented a paper to the Asiatick Society of Bengal, in which the British orientalist and jurist noted the obvious relationships among Sanskrit, Greek and Latin. He argued that the similarities were so pronounced that 'no philologer could examine them all three without believing them to have sprung from some common source which, perhaps, no longer exists'. Jones proposed the existence of an 'Indo-European' family, which would include Sanskrit, Greek, Latin, German and Celtic languages. The basic idea had been current for some time, and the term 'Indo-European' had been introduced a generation earlier, but now the insistence on a source variety linking geographically widespread languages was clearly stated. An historical approach to language classification, with its evolutionary tenor, was not novel in the century of Darwin's *Origin of Species*; so, as with the earlier linguistic analogues to herbals and bestiaries, language families were now viewed as products and reflections of evolutionary development.

Given the difficulties of accurate linguistic determination touched upon above, and to be further considered in the next chapter we can understand that accuracy in placing languages into families, and even in estimating the number of such families, is also difficult. The idea of the language 'family' is further complicated when we bear in mind the 'tree' metaphors that imply one original-language 'trunk' (or possibly a small number of such trunks: recall the note, above, about *monogenesis* and *polygenesis*); perhaps all languages are really relatives within one great 'super-family'. If we move upward and onward from an original trunk, however, it is easy to see that there is a very great deal of room for later classification: what one set of scholars might reasonably see as a family of closely linked branches, another set might consider to be a number of separate families, or perhaps sub-families. The large Indo-European family, for instance – all members of which may descend from an original 'Proto-Indo-European' trunk – has a number of sub-families, among the most important of which are the Germanic, Celtic, Hellenic and Italic subdivisions. Estimates of the number of contemporary language families, then, range widely: perhaps as few as 100, perhaps as many as 300.

The greatest number of speakers (about 2.5 billion) is found among the 450 Indo-European languages. The Niger-Congo and Austronesian families are much smaller (each with about 350 million speakers), but contain much greater language diversity: there are more than 1,500 languages in the former, and almost 1,300 in the latter. Other important assemblages include the Afro-Asiatic and Sino-Tibetan families. Drawing on several relevant sources a decade ago, I suggested an upper estimate of the number of English speakers (mother-tongue speakers and all others, considered together) to be about 1,400 million. This figure placed English ahead of Chinese (with about 1,000 million speakers) and well ahead of Hindi, in third place with 700 million speakers. My figure was seen in some quarters to be too high, but later analyses have borne it out. David Crystal now puts the figure at about 1,500 million, which 'suggests that approximately one in four of the world's population are now capable of communicating to a useful level in English'. Actual numbers aside, there can surely be little disagreement with Crystal's simple observation that 'there has never been a language so widely spread or spoken by so many people as English.'

For some languages, it has proved impossible to give an accurate classification: these varieties are known as 'language isolates'. This is true for ancient varieties known only because of references in classical literature: besides the Cappadocian to which I shall return (below), there are languages such as Bithynian and Pontic about which we know next to nothing. Ainu, the language of a group in Japan who are physically unlike the Japanese themselves, is a modern example of a variety that won't quite fit with others, as are the languages of the Salish and Kootenay peoples of British Columbia. So, too, is the now-extinct language of the Beothuks in Newfoundland. This society was ruthlessly slaughtered by Europeans, with the assistance of Indian mercenaries from the mainland, and the last speaker died of disease in St John's in 1829. It is ironic that this tribe should have been the one to prompt the generic term 'Red Indian': when John Cabot (Giovanni Caboto) first encountered them in the late fifteenth century, he observed and reported their custom of rubbing themselves with red ochre.

Modern Basque is also an isolate, thought to be a relic of pre-Indo-European Europe. Like the Ainu, the Basques are genetically different from their neighbours, and such biological classification provides data that supplement language-family assessments and speculations. If the speakers of Basque were already living in their mountains before those great immigrant waves from the east arrived, what could be more reasonable than to expect that they would be both linguistically and biologically different from their European neighbours? Similar triangulations between linguistic and genetic scholarship have reinforced classifications of cultural communities in other parts of the world too.

# CHAPTER TWO

# Interpreting Language Diversity

We must expand a little upon the lack of knowledge that makes counting and categorizing languages so difficult. At the most basic level, we find that language surveys are non-existent or incomplete in many parts of the world. Even in 'developed' societies, language census information is notoriously unreliable (see also Chapter 4). Sometimes, this means that languages are 'missed' altogether and, sometimes, the scope of known varieties becomes confused. The Canadian census of 1951 reported 14,000 speakers of Scottish Gaelic, a figure that dropped to 7,500 a decade later, but then, in 1971, re-emerged as 21,400. Did Gaelic fade away, only to return half again stronger than it was 20 years earlier? The answer is no. For that 1971 count, *all* Celtic languages other than Welsh were lumped in with the Gaelic figures.

## Dead or Alive

Insufficient linguistic knowledge often falls into several, quite specific categories. For instance, if we do not always have accurate basic information, it follows that we cannot be sure if a language continues to be spoken. Languages are vulnerable to social, political and economic changes affecting their users. These factors take their greatest toll, of course, among small or endangered languages and these, in turn, are often the ones we knew least about to begin with. (I shall return to the problems of declining languages in Chapters 9 and 10.) Sometimes, we know more or less exactly about the last speakers of a language. Dolly Pentreath, reputedly the last speaker of Cornish, died more than two centuries ago. Ned Maddrell was the last native speaker of Manx when he died in 1974. In 1985, researchers found that 82-year-old Tevfik Esenc was the last speaker of Oubykh (a language of the Caucasus).

A recent and very typical case is that of Marie Smith Jones, who died in January 2008 at the age of 89. She grew up on the Copper River delta in Alaska, and was the last person fluent in Eyak, a North American language related to the larger Athapaskan family. Her death, and that of her language, was noted in the media around the world, with the BBC and the (American) National Public Radio network providing audio commentaries and *The Economist* an excellent written one. All seemed to be galvanized by this event – the first indigenous Alaskan language to become extinct in recent times – although the death of vernacular varieties is hardly uncommon. Michael Krauss, who worked closely with Mrs Smith Jones and who has interested himself in endangered languages generally (see below), has suggested that, on average, a language is 'lost' every fortnight.

Eyak once flourished in southern Alaska, but rapidly lost ground in the twentieth century, coming to be spoken only in Eyak itself, a village now part of the town of Cordova. A commonly reported pattern in the settings of language decline involves a big language (like English) gradually ousting a smaller one (like Eyak). In many instances, however, this pattern is too simplistic. When Angela Sidney died, in 1991, she was considered to have been the last fluent speaker of Tagish; however, before Tagish had really begun to shrink under pressure from English, it had already been threatened, largely through trade and inter-marriage, by Tlingit. The same Tlingit

INTERPRETING LANGUAGE DIVERSITY

also pressured Eyak, as did Alutiiq and other varieties spoken in and around the Copper River country. And now Tlingit, too, is severely endangered, with only about 150 speakers, all of them bilingual (with English).

When Smith Jones was born, in 1918, there were perhaps 50 speakers left and, as a teenager, she began to encounter the odd anthropologist and folklorist, eager to capture something of what was obviously a dying language. At school, Eyak was either discouraged or forbidden, and it had no place in the fish cannery where Smith Jones worked. She herself was apparently unconcerned about Eyak, married outside her community, and found that her children had no interest in the language. It was only about a decade ago that she became something of a language activist, having finally realized the precarious state of her mother tongue. Dismissive of most white outsiders who came to interview her, Smith Jones began to work closely with Krauss, helping him to produce an Eyak grammar and dictionary.

There are important generalizable features that we can extract from the Eyak 'case'. Indeed, it is worth mentioning at this point that, while all language settings are unique, the uniqueness of each does not stem from the presence of elements that are found nowhere else in the world. On the contrary, there are many recurring aspects of language-contact situations. In fact, anyone who has ever attempted to compare and contrast across linguistic and cultural communities, or who has cited different examples to make a general point, has in effect argued that some features are constant or at least similar enough across contexts to suggest useful generalization. In other words, the uniqueness of each 'case' arises from specific weightings and arrangements of familiar features: a kaleidoscopic assortment of possibilities that are constructed, nevertheless, from a finite set of features.

Here are some of the important descriptions that we find, over and over again, in our studies of the social life of language. The first and most obvious is that languages are in dynamic relationships with one another; very often, these relationships are asymmetrical in terms of power and status. A language can falter, then, when in the shadow of stronger neighbours. In today's world, it is clear that this influence need not be geographically local: English, for instance, makes its presence felt from Afghanistan to Zimbabwe. Indeed, the power of the really big languages –of lingua francas like Greek, Arabic and Latin – has *never* been restricted to purely local neighbourhoods. An important corollary is that overweening linguistic neighbours need not always be large-language communities; they can be quite small local languages and dialects, very likely to encounter their own contact difficulties with larger varieties. Consider the Tagish-Tlingit-English nexus I touched upon earlier or the complexities of influence among African languages in contact.

A second generalizable point is that schools and other formal institutions often discourage the use of indigenous languages. This sometimes arises from prejudice or ignorance, but it usually involves at least some sense of what is considered the best for the children. However misguided and unfair we might think this to be, it has been a very common phenomenon around the world and one in which parents have often acquiesced. Again, many may see this as a regrettable occurrence, perhaps reflecting deep social inequities, lack of choice and so on. Nonetheless, even if schools promote a small language, and even if parents are brought to realize that stable bilingualism might represent a workable combination of large and small varieties, the fact that the latter increasingly find little applicability in the wider world also works against their preservation. More generally, we find that bilingualism in the declining language and its powerful linguistic neighbour is often only a temporary phenomenon, to be ultimately replaced by dominant-language monolingualism.

Third, interest in and concern for declining languages often arrive very late in the day, both personally and socially. Mrs Smith Jones was not prompted to action until she, too, was in her declining years. Languages in decline typically have a predominance of middle-aged or elderly speakers, and there is a lack of transmission to the younger generation. It is common to hear language revivalists express the wish that efforts had been put in train earlier. If only we had acted sooner to maintain Manx or Cornish, if only those immigrant languages of the new world had been encouraged and not subjected to anglicizing pressure, if only more scholars had been activists and advocates, and less like Matthew Arnold, whose historical and antiquarian interests in Celtic literature co-existed with a desire for the disappearance of spoken vernaculars and for the cultural assimilation of their speakers. If only we had more linguists like Michael Krauss and fewer ones who seem to prefer their languages safely dead, like Dickens's Miss Blimber.

> She was dry and sandy with working in the graves of deceased languages. None of your live languages for Miss Blimber. They must be dead – stone dead – and then Miss Blimber dug them up like a Ghoul.

It is perhaps an irony that representatives of the larger cultures that have brought about the demise of local languages are generally the ones to (finally) pay some consistent attention to them. Among other things, this accounts for the love-hate relationship that typically exists between members of indigenous communities and the 'outsiders', however committed they may be, who come to study and record their languages and cultures. Relatedly, we often find that *active* desires to stem the decline of threatened languages are very much a minority interest; indeed, revivalists are often non-group members who have become apologists for language maintenance. There is nothing intrinsically wrong with this, of course, and there are often very good reasons why 'ordinary' group members are unwilling or unable to take on active roles in linguistic and cultural defence. Still, when thinking about future linguistic fortunes, it is clear that there are important differences between leaders and followers – just as there are, more broadly speaking, important differences between native speakers and those who study and learn the language on a more self-conscious or voluntary basis. (Further notes on language decline and revival will be found in the final three chapters.)

If we began this list of common features with the observation that languages are typically in dynamic relationships with one another, we could add in conclusion that language change, rather than stasis, is the historical pattern and that ordinary people are largely motivated by practical necessity in linguistic matters. But in all considerations of cultural contact, we should never lose sight of the fact that language decline (or growth, of course) can be understood properly only as a *symptom* of group interaction, only as a consequence of inequalities at the points where communities meet. The logical conclusion – but one that often seems to be missed, ignored or denied in the literature of language maintenance and revival – is that efforts directed towards language preservation alone are unlikely to have a great deal of substantial or durable success. Much more radical intervention in the broad social fabric would seem necessary; many more changes would seem to be called for. Such revolutionary action is rare (and no doubt should be), but in communities in which language is an integral part of social evolution (that is to say, in *all* communities), surely a thoroughgoing reweaving of the societal fabric is the necessary underpinning of longstanding linguistic maintenance or alteration. And this is exactly the nub of the matter, because, in the vast majority of instances in which some language realignments are sought, the beneficiaries don't *want* to give up most of the other aspects of social life with which they have become familiar. It is doubtful, on both practical and theoretical grounds, whether such selectivity is feasible.

To end this list a little more positively, at least in terms of cultural continuity, we can note that while language shift has been and continues to be the norm for many small language communities – and historically, of course, for many larger ones, too – a case can be made that cultural integrity can be maintained despite language shift. This is a much larger topic than can be dealt with here, but scholars have argued that it is the maintenance of a sense of community boundaries that is required for the continuity of a sense of unique 'groupness'. The cultural 'stuff' that is found within the borders, however, and which sustains them, is mutable. In fact, the single most important prop of groupness is a continuing psychological awareness of membership, typically based upon conceptions (whether accurate or not) of shared ancestry. It is thus interesting to consider that the strongest of all cultural buttresses is the most intangible.

In terms of language, we note a distinction between communicative and symbolic aspects, between ordinary usage and the place of language as a marker of group identity. For majority-group speakers in settings in which they are dominant, both aspects generally coexist: the language in which you do your shopping, talk to your children or go to the pub is also the language of your group ancestry, the variety in which your history, poetry and legend are recorded. But the aspects can become separated, and minority-group speakers who are no longer able to use *their* ancestral language for ordinary communicative purposes often retain an attachment that involves the language as a group symbol. This can be valuable even when that language is no longer widely spoken, perhaps not known at all in some instances. I am not suggesting that a 'retreat' to symbolism is the first choice for those in small or threatened communities, either for ordinary group members or, more pointedly, for activists and revivalists. I am also not arguing for its broader desirability in any disinterested discussion. I am simply pointing out that such a 'retreat' will likely continue to be a feature of life in many settings and that – intangible though language-as-symbol is – it is both incorrect and condescending to dismiss what continues to be psychologically relevant in the lives of many people.

Revivalists may bewail the fact that intervention in language decline is often a matter of 'too little, too late', but we have ample evidence from all sorts of human arenas that things often have to grow to perilous proportions before substantial movement is galvanized. Hindsight is a great thing here, as elsewhere. In fact, even ascertaining the point of actual language *death* is not always easy and, obviously, the difficulty increases as we go back further in time. As already noted, the existence of some ancient varieties is confirmed only through classical reference: Cappadocian once thrived in what is now central Turkey, but we know next to nothing about it. There are also undeciphered varieties. We have thousands of examples of Etruscan texts, but the brevity of many inscriptions (most are funerary) and the 'isolate' nature of the language (there are only two other languages in the family, Lemnian and Rhaetic, and neither is well attested) mean that our understanding of Etruscan is incomplete. Still, Etruscan seems not quite so dead as Cappadocian. But consider the possibility of further archaeological discoveries at the famous Kerkenes excavations, east of Ankara, discoveries that might very well lead to increased knowledge of Cappadocian. Is it possible that a dead language could then be brought back to some sort of life? As for those 'dead' languages that students sometimes moan about – Latin and Attic Greek – well, they don't seem very dead at all in this company. There appear to be degrees of linguistic mortality.

In any event, we probably shouldn't think of Latin as a dead language at all. The Vatican still makes pronouncements in that language, of course, and dictionaries published under its auspices remain remarkably up to date. In *Latinitas Nova et Vetera*, for example, one will discover *escarorium lavator* (washing machine), *exterioris pagine puella* (cover girl) and *serpentinus cursus* (football dribbling). Providing the only service to rival that of the Vatican, Radio Finland began to broadcast a Latin news bulletin in 1989. What began as a publicity effort for its international programming soon became a more serious venture, heard around the world on the shortwave band. Professor Tuomo Pekkanen presented a 'lean and economical' Latin, free of circumlocutions: while 'television' could be described as a *machina ad vim electricam trasmittendam ita instructa ut sine intervallo imagines ac voces e longinquo indicet*, Pekkanen suggested *televistrum* (a Greek-Latin hybrid). Another Finnish professor, Jukka Ammondt, now sings Elvis songs in Latin; his repertoire includes *Nunc hic aut numquam* ('It's now or never'), *Ne saevias* ('Don't be cruel') and *Glaudi calcei* ('Blue suede shoes'). This is just language play, to be sure, but it makes an important point: all languages, whatever their age and condition, can be adapted to new requirements.

We can now track the status of languages more accurately than ever before, and it is fair to say that there is greater interest nowadays in preserving linguistic diversity. Heightened attention, however, does not ensure prolonged life. There are 53 surviving aboriginal languages in Canada, and most are well documented. But only three (Inuktitut, Ojibwa and Cree) are considered to have a good chance of survival; Cree is the strongest but even it has only about 60,000 regular speakers. All of the other fifty are seen to be endangered; half of those have fewer than 500 speakers. The fortunes of Han, an Athapaskan language spoken in Alaska and the Yukon by fewer than ten elderly people, are illustrative here. A population of several hundred at the beginning of the twentieth century was reduced by smallpox, typhus and other diseases, so that by the 1930s only about 60 people were left. The Han population has since recovered to perhaps 400, but the language has not.

# The Problem of Names

If grappling with issues of decline and death is one important manifestation of lack of linguistic knowledge, then the 'naming problem' is another. This difficulty arises because a language is often given different designations. The Oubykh language, whose last speaker was Tevfik Esenc, for example, is also called Ubykh or Ubyx. Multiple names are of course particularly likely to occur for remote and small varieties, but even better-known languages may have several names. As well, the different names for the same variety are not always similar: a connection among Oubykh, Ubykh and Ubyx might be guessed, but that language has *also* been called Pekhi. A few other examples will illustrate these points: in South Africa, Fanagolo is also known as Isikula, Silunguboi and Cilololo; in Turkey, Circassian is also Adygey and Cherkes; Atruahi, Jawaperi and Waimiri are names for the same Brazilian language; in North America, Gwichin, Loucheux, Tukudh and Kutchin refer to the same aboriginal variety.

Multiple names arise for a number of reasons. Different writing systems and conventions will complicate matters, of course: just a small variation (as between Ubykh and Oubykh) may lead to problems of indexing and categorization. The names of different sub-groups, tribes or clans may all become attached to a language held in common. Different groups of 'foreigners' – whether adjacent language communities, explorers or invaders or scholars of different nationalities – may have their own names for the same people and language.

The 'naming' problem can prove very difficult, even for countries with considerable census expertise and penetration. As Bhadranna Mallikarjun has put it, 'caste names, names of clans, names of professions, names of religious sects, names of speech or language not currently in use, names of villages, regions or provinces, names of animals and birds, and a host of other names may be offered as the name of the language of the individual being counted under the census'. (This is to say nothing, of course, of the great possibilities for confusion between languages and dialects.) And he goes on to add that 'only the so-called educated persons, living in their own world of knowledge, wisdom and cynicism, think that every individual in India knows the name of the language he or she speaks'. While we are told that increased attempts are being made to 'rationalize' the names of the mother tongues recorded in the census, there also remains 'some complacency, and an unwillingness to recognize the possibility of the diversity of responses'. The upshot is that in the famous 1961 Indian census, there were 1,652 mother tongues reported, but just over 400 languages.

Group names can be remarkably informative. Some are very easy to understand: geographical variants of the 'people-of-the-river' or 'the-mountain-dwellers' sort are common, for example. Self-descriptions also often suggest that those outside the group are qualitatively different: many communities style themselves with some synonym or equivalent of the pronoun 'we'. This seems innocuous enough, and not unreasonable, perhaps, when groups live in relative isolation from others, when inter-group contact is rare or fleeting. However, it is a little disturbing to realize that one of those variants of 'we' or 'us' is 'the people', with the implication that those beyond the group boundaries are not fully or adequately human. Such names are found in many parts of the world, among groups as widely separated as (for example) the Ainu, Bantu, Berber, Blackfoot, Chuchi, Inuit, Iroquois, Kaluli, Kannaka, Maya, Navajo, Nez Percé, Roma, Salish, Sámi, Tsimshian and Washoe communities. Many of those who self-identify as 'the people' extend their selectivity to what they speak, too: 'the real language' is what the Tsimshian (and many others) speak.

Further interesting refinements also occur. Sometimes, 'the people' becomes something like 'the best people', 'the first people' (Chippewa and Ojibwe) or, simply, 'the human beings' (Cherokee). While terms like 'Blackfoot' and 'Nez Percé' should not, perhaps, be interpreted as anything more than rough external appellations, some of the Dakota ('the friends') became known as Sioux ('snakes'), an abbreviation of a term bestowed upon them by enemies. Many Inuit consider the earlier term 'Eskimo' to be a derogatory reference to them as eaters of raw meat. While the Welsh call themselves *Cymry* (meaning something like 'fellow countrymen'), the English name for them derives from the Anglo-Saxon *w(e)alh*, via the Germanic *Wälsche* ('stranger', 'foreigner' or even 'barbarian'). The Khoisan speakers of southern Africa call themselves *Khoekhoe* – 'men of men' – but the Dutch called them 'Hottentots' (stutterers). In seventeenth-century Muscovy, foreigners were called *nemtsy* ('mutes'), a Russian labelling now restricted to Germans. A particularly egregious example is found among the Asmat of Irian Jaya: while they are 'the human beings', they classify everyone else as *manowe*: the 'edible ones'. Such ethnic naming conventions are also found, of course, in religiously based groups. Some interpretations within Islam divide the world into those within the sacred 'house' and those without, and the Christian bible echoes with racism, with accounts that describe the 'other' as impure, unclean, idolatrous, evil and depraved.

A further complicating factor in the matter of names is the confusion between language and dialect. Strictly speaking, a dialect is a sub-variety of a language that differs from other varieties in its vocabulary, grammar and pronunciation (accent). Being forms of the same language, dialects are mutually intelligible, where languages are not: French speakers cannot understand Fanagolo speakers, but Texans can understand Londoners. Everyone realizes, of course, that mutual intelligibility among dialects is often more theoretical than real; everyone has heard dialects of their own language that are almost impossible to understand.

Mutual intelligibility falters at another level, too. Consider a *dialect continuum*, along which lie varieties A, B, C and D. Speakers of dialect A can easily understand B, can just follow C, but cannot comprehend D. Are A and D then different languages, even though C and D speakers understand one another, even though a chain of intelligibility exists from A through to D? Such continua are in fact quite common: dialects of German and Dutch form such a chain, as do varieties of Slovak, Czech, Ukrainian, Polish and Russian, or Romance dialects of Italian, French, Catalan, Spanish and Portuguese.

We must also bear in mind here issues of political allegiance, national identity and power: as Max Weinreich once said, 'a language is a dialect that has an army and navy'. Cantonese and Mandarin speakers may have considerable difficulty understanding one another but they are considered to speak dialects of Chinese, not only because they use the same written form, but also because of the overarching state of which they are members. On the other hand, Norwegian and Danish speakers can understand each other well, but the demands of national and political identity require that they have 'different' languages. There are other examples, too, of the dominance of political concerns over purely linguistic ones, concerns that dictate that Hindi and Urdu, Flemish and Dutch, Serbian and Croatian are to be seen as separate languages.

The last pair provides us with a particularly powerful, if repellent, example of the influence of identity politics upon language. Once upon a time, there was a language called Serbo-Croatian, a common variety among not just Serbs and Croats, but also Bosnians and Montenegrins. Although there were regional and dialectal variants, and a number of contentious historical, orthographical and grammatical points, Serbo-Croatian was a widely accepted medium since the mid-nineteenth century. Towards the end of the twentieth century, however, the language began to feel political pressures; sentiment in some Croat quarters, for instance, held that it was too 'Serbianized' a medium. Now, in a post-Yugoslavian era, we find that Serbo-Croatian no longer has an official existence: it has been replaced by Bosnian, Serbian and Croatian. What has actually happened, linguistically? In Serbia, very little. In Bosnia, moves to emphasize Arabic-Turkish features have been made, but basic grammar and lexicon have been little affected. In Croatia, however, symbolic declarations have been accompanied by 'a campaign to actually make the language as different from Serbian (or Serbo-Croatian) as possible, and as quickly as possible.' Active moves currently being made to drive instrumental wedges, to try and make two languages where once only one existed – these surely highlight the political importance of linguistic group markers. It is disappointing to realize that, as part of the *realpolitik* of language planning, scholars are at this moment setting up barriers to communication under the flag of group solidarity.

# CHAPTER THREE

# Multilingual Abilities

## Multilingualism in the World

Multilingualism is both a simple description of global linguistic diversity and, at the same time, a representation of the individual and group abilities that have developed because of that very diversity. Since languages are many and life is short, there have always existed important lingua francas that serve as aids to cross-group communication. These have typically been the languages of potent and prestigious societies: Greek, Latin, French, Spanish, Arabic and, currently, English have all held sway at one time or another. The strong and obvious attractions of lingua francas have historically coexisted with, and not eliminated, more local varieties. They have not spelled the death of multilingualism so much as they have been a product of it and, indeed, a contributor to it. Serious questions are now being raised, however, about the linguistically 'murderous' potential of the English language (see also Chapter 8).

Beyond the use of languages that cross community borders, individual multilingual abilities are also common necessities in most parts of the world – common and, in most instances, normal and quite unremarkable. It is both a fact and a frequent lament, however, that speakers of big languages lag far behind others in foreign-language competence. A reasonable corollary is that, at a social level, such competence is inversely proportional to the 'bigness' of the mother tongue: contemporary anglophone populations are among the very poorest of language learners. Language teaching in English-speaking countries is more difficult and less attractive than in Europe. Do we observe here some genetic anglophone linguistic deficiency? Are the British and the Americans right when they say, 'I'm just no good at foreign languages'? Are they right to envy those clever Africans, Europeans and Asians who slide effortlessly from one mode to another? The answers here obviously involve environmental conditions, not genetic ones – once upon a time, anglophones were excellent language learners – but I present these silly notions because they constitute in some quarters a type of self-fulfilling prophecy that adds to the difficulty of language learning. I use the word 'adds' here because the real difficulties, the important contextual conditions, the soil in which such prophecies flourish, have to do with power and dominance. Contemporary anglophone linguistic laments often involve some crocodile tears or, at least, are rather hollow: they represent the superficial regrets of those who lack competence, but who need not, after all, really bother to acquire it. The world is increasingly being made safe for anglophones, and readers may like to consider whether this is a good thing, a bad thing, an inevitable thing, a reversible thing, and so on.

At state or regional levels, we find a number of responses to linguistic heterogeneity. The most general of these is to elevate only one variety to official status. With about 4,500 languages in some 200 countries, internal linguistic heterogeneity is obviously the norm. Still, only a quarter of those countries recognize more than one language. In states where two or more varieties have official or legal status, one language is usually predominant, or has regional limitations, or carries with it disproportionate amounts of social, economic and political power. Switzerland, for example, with its recognition of German, French, Italian and Romansch, shows clear linguistic dominance for one variety at the canton level and the four languages are not, in any event, anything like equal in cross-community utility. Singapore also has four official languages (English, Mandarin, Tamil and Malay) but the latter two are much less important than the former pair. Ireland recognizes both Irish and English as national varieties, but the first has only symbolic significance in the general life of the country. *Und so weiter.*

Whether officially recognized or not, linguistic heterogeneity need not correlate with expanded personal capabilities. In India, Hindi is the first official language, English is co-official, and the government also recognizes 22 other 'scheduled' languages as official (refraining, however, from specifying a single pan-Indian *national* variety). And beyond this, as we have seen already, lies a much richer linguistic landscape: more than 400 languages, categorized into the Indo-Aryan, Dravidian, Austric and Tibeto-Burman families. Like India, Nigeria is linguistically very rich – richer, perhaps, when one considers that its 500 languages are distributed among a population that, at about 155 million, is only about one-eighth the size of India's. Unlike India, however, Nigeria's sole official language is English; Hausa, Ibo and Yoruba are also acknowledged nationally, and half a dozen other languages have regional recognition. Regardless of numbers of languages, whether 'official' or otherwise, it is easy to predict *both* widespread multilingualism *and* widespread monolingualism in these sorts of settings. Some speakers may spend their entire lives within essentially monolingual enclaves. Others may range rather more widely and broaden their linguistic repertoires, but only to the minimal degrees necessitated by repetitive and routine encounters. And still others may develop deep and substantial fluencies in several languages. As always, circumstances will alter cases.

The generality is this: multilingual competence is clearly necessary in many settings, but the fact that these settings vary in terms of speakers, topics and requirements implies that linguistic capabilities are not equally developed. In fact, given the complexities here, and the social exigencies attached to various types of interaction, it would not be very sensible to 'overdevelop' language fluencies. Except among those for whom repertoire expansion is a goal in and of itself, language competence typically extends only as far as current requirements dictate. In situations where more than one language is involved, different forms often intertwine for different purposes. This is a phenomenon well known to students of *code-switching*, where individuals change languages frequently, often within one sentence.

Here is an excerpt of a conversation between two Mexican Americans on the subject of cigarette smoking:

> Tu no fumas, verdad? Yo tampoco. Deje de fumar and I'm back to it again…. Se me acababan los cigarros en la noche. I'd get desperate, y ahi voy al basurero a buscar, a sacar, you know?

Code-switching now has a large literature to itself, and one or two general points can be extracted from it here. First, language 'switches' are typically non-random: in the full conversation between the speakers (above), Spanish was used when they seemed embarrassed about their smoking, English when making more impersonal remarks. Second, while *interference* between languages may make its presence felt in code-switching, particularly where the norms of one language are incorrectly applied to another, the more neutral *transference* is generally a better description. Speakers will often switch for emphasis, because they feel that the *mot juste* is found more readily in one of their languages than in another, or because of their perceptions of the speech situation, changes in content, the linguistic skills of their interlocutors, degrees of intimacy and so on.

In some ears, code-switching is heard unfavourably as, indeed, are any language mixtures: terms like Spanglish, Denglish, Franglais and Japlish are generally used pejoratively. Even bilingual speakers themselves have reported feeling embarrassed at their 'impure' utterances, a sad commentary on how easy it is to internalize ignorant and prejudicial attitudes. The truth of the matter, after all, is that unlike monolinguals, who also 'switch' constantly among registers and styles, but must obviously do so within the confines of a single language, multilinguals have an even wider repertoire to draw upon, and it is hard to see that this is anything but useful.

## Individual Attitudes and Abilities

Multilingualism is a world phenomenon, but since official or prestige status is often restricted, it is clear that attitudes towards multilingualism and language diversity in general are important. At socially élite levels, multilingualism has always been encouraged and has, in itself, been a marker of high status. In the middle ages, those European scholars, diplomats and aristocrats who spoke languages other than their mother tongue enjoyed a level of education and privilege light years removed from the lives of the masses. Not to have known Latin or Greek or French in addition to one's vernacular would have been unthinkable, but often unthinkable, perhaps, in the same way that it would have been unthinkable not to have had servants. The use of French in the royal courts of Europe is an obvious reflection of linguistic élitism. In Sobieski's Polish court, in Catherine's St Petersburg, in Frederick's Berlin and in many other royal quarters from the seventeenth century onwards, French was the language of aristocratic prestige. Thus, while visiting the court of Frederick II, his friend and correspondent, Voltaire wrote that it was just like being in France: 'on ne parle que notre langue. L'allemand est pour les soldats et pour les chevaux; il n'est nécessaire que pour la route.'

There have always been language prejudices and preferences. The sixteenth-century Holy Roman Emperor is supposed to have neatly distributed his various language fluencies: he spoke Spanish to God, Italian to women, French to men and German to horses. In the seventeenth century, Richard Carew described

Italian as 'pleasant', French 'delicate', Spanish 'majestic' and Dutch 'harsh but virile': none could compare, however, to the excellence of English. And, in the eighteenth century, Antoine Rivarol said that 'ce qui n'est pas clair n'est pas français' and he went on to nominate English, Italian, Greek and Latin. And so it goes. Today, while there may be fewer who are quite so ready to lionize one *language* while castigating others, criticism at the level of *dialect* (which also has a long history) remains common, demonstrating that preferential inclinations have hardly abated. In his *Arte of English Poesie*, published in 1589, George Puttenham argued that the best English was home-counties English. Four centuries later, Robert Chapman and Henry Wyld, well-known scholars both, were still claiming that standard or 'received' English was the best of dialects. And, today, there are many who have strong, if inaccurate and ill-informed, views about the poverty of non-standard varieties – like one of the teachers I interviewed a few years ago, who told me that her black students had 'a slang language all their own. They will not use proper English when opportunity arises'. Another teacher reported that 'these poor kids come to school speaking a hodge podge'. And these are the views of *teachers*, remember.

Such opinions reflect prevailing social attitudes and, as I have noted, say nothing about intrinsic qualities, either of languages or, as is often implied, of the cognitive skills of their speakers. Nonetheless, the power behind such opinions has often meant that difference has been translated into deficit. This is the most important point: regardless of the state of scholarly enlightenment, social pressures have always had powerful consequences, regardless of the accuracy of the attitudes underpinning them. Or, as Bill Mackey noted a few years ago: 'only before God and the linguist are all languages equal.'

In terms of individual capabilities, the general historical consensus has been that the more languages one speaks, the better. Roger Bacon, the *Doctor Mirabilis* of the thirteenth century, correlated multilingualism with wisdom. Charles V, the same sixteenth-century emperor already cited here, pointed out that *quot linguas calles, tot homines vales*: one is worth as many people as languages known. This sentiment can be found in proverbial expressions around the world, in fact. Still, there have always been dissenting opinions. John Milton argued that knowledge of several languages was not, in itself, a marker of expanded wisdom or insight, and Samuel Butler was rather more pointed: 'the more languages a man can speak, his talent has but sprung the greater leak.'

This debate continues today, particularly noticeable in the literature dealing with the relationship between bilingualism and intelligence. In the modern era, early research implied that bilinguals (and multilinguals, of course) paid some sort of cognitive price for their expanded language repertoire, while later findings tend to suggest either no particular correlation or a moderately positive one. The relevant literature is a large and often technical one, and I restrict myself here to three related points. First, findings are often bedevilled by the old admonition that correlation is not the same as causation: are those who become bilingual smarter than others to begin with, or does a wider repertoire enhance intelligence? Many efforts have been made to control this matter, but *experimenta cruces* are hard to fashion. Second, while most people around the world are bilingual or better, there seems not to be any great evidence linking these expanded fluencies with greater basic knowledge or insight. Those bilinguals who are studied in the literature are generally a rather special subset of this global population: they live in 'developed' societies where their abilities, either present or nascent, tend to stand out, they are literate and educated, they are relatively well-off, and so on. Third, whatever the verdict may turn out to be, it is impossible to deny that, for most people most of the time, the expansion of linguistic repertoires must be a good and useful thing.

In some cases, this expansion has been quite remarkable. There are prodigies in language just as there are in music and mathematics. In 1866, James Murray, twenty-nine years old and destined to be the first editor of the *Oxford English Dictionary*, applied for a post in the British Museum Library. He wrote the following:

> I possess a general acquaintance with the languages and literature of the Aryan and Syro-Arabic classes ... with several [languages] I have a more intimate acquaintance, as with the Romance tongues, Italian, French, Catalan, Spanish, Latin and in a less degree Portuguese, Vaudois, Provençal and various dialects. In the Teutonic branch I am tolerably familiar with Dutch ... Flemish, German, Danish. In Anglo-Saxon and Moeso-Gothic my studies have been much closer ... I know a little of the Celtic, and am at present engaged with the Sclavonic [sic], having obtained a useful knowledge of Russian. In the Persian, Achaemenian Cuneiform and Sanscrit [sic] branches, I know for the purposes of Comparative Philology. I have sufficient knowledge of Hebrew and Syriac to read at sight the OT [Old Testament] ... to a less degree I know Aramaic Arabic, Coptic and Phenician [sic].

The famous Victorian explorer, Richard Francis Burton, travelled extensively in India, Arabia, North and South America. He too seems to have had a genius for language, claiming to have developed his own acquisition techniques by which a few months' study could lead to mastery of a new variety. There is no doubt that Burton was competent in more than two dozen varieties. Remarkable though Murray and Burton were, particularly by anglophone standards, we should not imagine that such multiplication of capabilities is found only in exceptional cases. Paulin Djité, a friend and colleague of mine, grew up in Côte d'Ivoire speaking French and Wè at home and Yoruba, Baoulé and Dyula with playmates and others. His education was through French, English and Spanish. As an adolescent, he added Attié, Gouro, Koulango, Dida and Bété to his linguistic repertoire, along with a more passive knowledge of Ewe and other varieties. His language skills are formidable but, as he himself has pointed out, many educated Africans have followed similar linguistic paths.

Even among those whose fluencies are very extensive, most multilingual speakers begin with a particular mother tongue, a particular linguistic home camp. But there are some cases where home itself is difficult to establish. There are some cases, that is, where bilingual or multilingual capacities, linked to their several cultural bases, develop so early and so deeply that a primary allegiance is hard to discover. There are generally two ways to consider the situations of those whose bilingualism (or multilingualism) begins at the parental knees. The first is simply that two or more base camps are home simultaneously; the second is that one primary home indeed exists, but it is constructed, in a manner unique to the individual, from materials taken from the several sources. The writer and critic George Steiner has claimed early, continuing and more or less equal competence in German, French and English: perhaps a perfect trilingual. He reasonably suggests that such 'primary' multilingualism may have social and psychological implications quite different from those associated with sequential language acquisition. We have little information on this, but we can be sure that there are subtleties here that go far beyond simple additive relationships.

# Language as a Verb and Other Infelicities

Concerned as this little book is with the broadest outlines of multilingualism, I cannot do more than remind readers that the school is one of the most important settings in which varying language abilities come together. Responses to linguistic heterogeneity in the classroom have varied considerably over time and setting, and enlightenment has not made its way into all quarters. Still, whether dealing with separate languages or with dialects of the same language, it is not unreasonable to suggest that educational thinking has become more sensitive to variation, and more inclined to see it as a strength and a resource, rather than a difficulty to be overcome. On the one hand, this is part of a broader awareness of the legitimacy of *all* varieties, large or small, standard or non-standard. On the other, it is an acknowledgement that education is better conceived as the best possible 'fit' to children's backgrounds and needs than as a rigid and monolithic entity to which the latter must adapt. This thinking has underpinned specialized programmes, like bilingual and bicultural education – and there is a very large literature devoted to these – but some of its most recent expressions should be treated very cautiously. I hope that readers will share my dismay at the following description of egregious usage.

Some scholars now tell us that 'diversity' is a term no longer sufficient to cover social heterogeneity and that 'superdiversity' is more appropriate. This refers to an 'interweaving of diversities', a world of 'migrant transnationalism' and a world in which 'assimilation and enduring transnational ties are neither incompatible nor binary'. Relatedly, we are told that linguistic identities can be multifaceted: 'what exactly is wrong with linguistic complementarity?' What indeed – but what informed opinion ever denied that identities and the ways of expressing them can be many and varied? These and other similar observations have set up a series of straw men, which are then countered with unnecessary and – worse – confusing terms and arguments. 'Superdiversity' is an obviously unnecessary term, coined to suggest a non-existent development. Similarly, while I think that 'transnationalism', the continuing connectivity that links homeland and diaspora (for example), is indeed more common nowadays, it is hardly a new phenomenon. That degrees of assimilation exist with retention of older affiliations is not a novel observation, either.

All this is by way of background to discussions of 'languaging' and 'translanguaging.' It must be said, right away, that those guilty of using these ugly terms have remarkably stannous ears, a particularly unhappy circumstance, surely, for those who are language scholars. On a particularly critical day, I might be

tempted to suggest that those who write in this way have forfeited
any claim on our serious attention. (They certainly reinforce
the popular and, alas, often accurate image of the portentous
and pedantic academic.) 'Translanguaging' was apparently
first used in a Welsh school context in which pupils do their
work in a language other than that in which information was
presented to them. It was meant to be a broader concept than
code-switching (see above), signifying rather 'an arrangement
that normalizes bilingualism without diglossic functional
separation'. There is something to this, perhaps, although it is
unclear why a suitably qualified reference to code-switching
would not serve in such settings. But, just as the equally
rebarbative term 'languaging' has been unnecessarily coined to
refer to the many ways in which languages are used by people
in their 'multiple discursive practices', so 'translanguaging' now
seems to mean any and all types of cross-language switching,
stylistic variation, and so on.

The expressed need for educational policies that focus
on 'translingual language practices rather than language
entities' seems to suggest entirely reasonable school postures,
ones that take account of the varied and varying linguistic
backgrounds of children. However, as other similarly-minded
commentators point out, school children – like all speakers,
indeed – show 'playfulness and creativity' in their verbal
exchanges. Yet another researcher tells us that we need to
eliminate the 'whole language' myth (see below) and create new
linguistic visions that are 'more inclusive of differences, of the
translanguaging that is so extensive in bilingual communities
and classrooms'. In combination, then, these 'translanguaging'
advocates are suggesting that the linguistic dexterity which
we have known about for a long time, and which we have
explicitly acknowledged at least since the classic sociolinguistic
investigations of the 1960s, be reflected in school practices.
Hardly earth-shaking.

As just implied, those responsible for 'languaging' have
also called into question the very idea of languages; they
are inventions, particularly in the sense that they exist as

'separable and enumerable categories'. Writers who take this line grudgingly admit that, in some unenlightened quarters, the old idea of a language still remains: 'we are obliged to take account of what people believe about their languages ... even where we believe these "languages" to be inventions.' What at first blush seems the height of absurdity here is merely an attempt to be provocative. Languages and the identities with which they are associated are, of course, social constructions: 'inventions' if you like. Languages and language varieties, both across people and communities, as well as within individual linguistic repertoires, lack sharp boundaries: of course they do. But, again, this is nothing new.

More importantly, however, we have here an excellent example of how a divergence between (some) scholars and the broader public can reveal the latter to be more accurate. For all ordinary intents and purposes, there *are* separate languages, and there *are* distinct varieties within them. When we read that the idea of separate languages helps to 'perpetuate social inequities', however, we come closer to understanding why (some) scholars seem so intent on obfuscation. Only by 'disinventing', followed by a 'reinvention which acknowledges heterogeneity', can we alleviate these inequities. The naïveté here is striking, and it is a version of that same innocence or ignorance which fails to grasp that language shift is a symptom of larger social movements (a point that I have already touched upon, and to which I shall return). Of course, we should pay much closer attention to social inequality and to the part that language practices may play in it. Of course, we should understand that patterns of linguistic dominance and subordination are reprehensible and destructive. But it is simply wrong to state *tout court* that 'language classification' is a 'construct' aimed at controlling variety and difference, excluding 'mixed language practices, creoles and other ways of using languages in multilingual networks'.

There is no doubt that certain linguistic 'constructs' have had undesirable consequences, but so might any reworking, any attempt at encouraging 'translinguality.' Ultimately, *any* act of communication can be either elevated or condemned: this has to do with power, whatever the language in which it is expressed. We accept that most scholarship involves going back over well-ploughed ground, and this can be extremely valuable; indeed, the greater linguistic sensitivity that I mentioned at the beginning of this section is a case in point. But uncouth neologisms and dysfluent phrasings don't represent an advance. What we have in most of the relevant discussion are ham-handed reminders of Bakhtin's well-known arguments about 'heteroglossia', about the non-neutrality of language, about a polyphonic world, about language in the service of the social order and so on. None of this, incidentally, was new when Bakhtin wrote about it: any good study of the translation of fiction, for instance, will reveal the historically longstanding awareness of vocal multiplicities, their sources, their intertwinings and, consequently, the problems of interpretation that they present. These problems are evidences of the very 'translinguality' that is now being discussed as if were a new conceit; see also Chapter 6, below.

Finally here, we can note that some of the most general sentiments that apparently underlie the 'translingual' movement reveal important lapses of understanding. We are told, for instance, that we need analysis that 'takes account of plurality of affiliation, the coexistence of cohesion and separateness, and the fact that people cohere to different social worlds and communities simultaneously'. We are also reminded that 'the ability to language [sic] ... is the most important signifying role of human beings – that which gives life meaning.' Apart from the infelicitous phrasing, the first of these observations suggests an ignorance of the very well-known and long-established findings, from sociology and social psychology, bearing upon multiple social identities, roles and allegiances. The second manages to combine ugliness with a truly striking lack of psychological awareness.

I believe that the writers whose work I have cited here are well-meaning, but they are so maladroit that one doesn't know whether to laugh or cry. Jargon and neologism to no useful purpose. Pretentiousness and barren verbiage. Lack of novelty coupled with inelegant expression. I would be the last to deny that it is the special obligation of the scholar to probe for nuance in a world of blunt instruments, but success here requires care and sensitivity. The illusion of progress is worse than stasis, but the pressures within today's social-science research community – allied with the seductions of some vacuous elements of postmodernity – encourage work of the sort that I have criticized here. Thus, particularly in its insecure and weaker divisions, the academy often produces material of (at best) incestuous interest.

# CHAPTER FOUR

# The Emergence and Measurement of Multilingualism

## The Rise of Multilingualism

It is clear that multilingualism has always been a widespread global phenomenon. The religion and culture of Judaism provide an excellent historical case in point. Arthur Koestler described the descendants of the biblical tribes as representing 'the classic example of linguistic adaptability' and demonstrating how group identity can outlive communicative language shift.

> first they spoke Hebrew; in the Babylonian exile, Chaldean; at the time of Jesus, Aramaic; in Alexandria, Greek; in Spain, Arabic, but later Ladino – a Spanish-Hebrew mixture written in Hebrew characters, the Sephardi equivalent of Yiddish; and so it goes on. They preserved their religious identity, but changed languages at their convenience.

'At their convenience' seems a little glib, since people do not alter their linguistic habits lightly or without very good cause, but Koestler's example shows that language shift need not destroy a communal sense of historical and cultural continuity.

The rise of multilingualism and its ramifications are not difficult to understand. Immigrants to a new country obviously bring languages into contact, a common experience in all the new-world 'receiving' societies. Territorial expansion is another type of migration, with similar results. It is not always necessary for large numbers of people to physically move; their language may come into contact with others through military and economic pressures, requiring only a handful of soldiers, merchants and bureaucrats. A few thousand people ruling the Indian sub-continent brought about a massively expanded base for English among a (current) population of more than a billion. Some 100 million of these people can speak English, in addition to at least one other variety. Political union among different linguistic groups will also lead to multilingualism: those who once may have existed in sufficient isolation as not to need a broadened language ability may come to find themselves more closely united with other linguistic communities. Switzerland is an example already noted; Belgium is a country of French and Flemish speakers; Canada has English and French 'charter' groups. In addition to such unions, there are federations based upon more involuntary amalgamations: there are many examples of colonial boundary-marking and country-creation in Africa and Asia. Predictably enough, these formations are fraught with danger, and with hindsight we can see that imperialist politics left many delayed-action devices – some of them linguistic – buried in local fields. Besides the dialect continua already mentioned, multilingualism is also commonly observed in border areas. International borders *may* respect pre-existing linguistic divisions, they *may* respect and conform to long-established community distinctions, but they very often do not. Many boundaries have been established in circumstances in which local sensitivities and usages have not been consulted. Two North American examples can be found along the Mexican-American border in the south and on that between New England and Quebec in the north.

These are the most obvious reasons for the growth of multilingual competence. They are not, of course, the only ones: cultural and educational motivations will also expand linguistic repertoires, for example, even if there is no desire or possibility to use the new ability in ordinary conversational ways. Through the examples cited here, and perhaps even including those where purely scholarly factors are at work, there nevertheless runs a thread of necessity. A moral, then, which could be drawn, is that multilingualism is largely a practical affair, that few people become or remain multilingual on a whim, but also that, in almost all instances, an individual's abilities in his or her two, three or four languages will not be equally developed. On the contrary, as I implied earlier, we might predict that they will extend just as far as circumstances demand.

# Assessing Multilingualism

Whether or not a language is in some way or other recognized in legislation, many societies regularly assess the type and extent of multilingualism within their borders. This is an exercise useful in many ways: to better serve cultural and other needs, to identify the size and composition of specific groups for specific purposes, to gauge the depth and variety of available language skills within national and regional borders, to fine-tune present and future immigration policies, to measure the results of language maintenance or revivalist policies, to assist in targeted marketing, and so on.

This information is most commonly collected by census, although census data are often limited and sometimes downright misleading (as we have seen in Chapter 2). An initial difficulty arises in the phrasing of questions. Should we ask respondents to tell us their mother tongue? If so, how do we know that all informants will interpret 'mother tongue' in the same way? And what of those Steiners among us who feel they have more than one mother tongue, or of those who have forgotten or never use their maternal variety? Further confusion arises when questions, definitions and instructions for respondents alter over time. Canadian censuses up to 1941 defined mother tongue as the language first learned and still spoken. From 1941 to 1976, it was the language first spoken and still understood and, in 1981, respondents were asked about the language first learned and still understood. Mother tongue has had other descriptions, too: in some national censuses, it has been defined as the language spoken in the person's home when he or she was a child; in this case, a 'mother tongue' might never have been actually learned by the informant. Some of the distinctions – perhaps that between 'first spoken' and 'first learned' – may seem unimportant, but anyone who has had anything to do with the development and interpretation of questionnaire date will be alive to the smallest nuance. The general point, of course, is simply that *any* change in wording (or, of course, in the way questions are actually presented to informants: in the Canadian census of 1961, enumerators were used, while a decade later it was purely a self-reported effort) can alter responses in important but usually unmeasurable ways.

Perhaps we should ask simpler questions, perhaps something like 'what is the first language you spoke?' But, as with the apparently more fraught enquiries about the language learned at the maternal knee, this may not provide us with the information we would most like to have. If we want to know about languages currently spoken, for instance, asking about mother tongues or 'first' languages will clearly not always serve. In at least some instances, then, we might simply ask people about the language they now speak most often. This sort of enquiry also raises difficulties. How, for instance, will it be answered by those who speak two or more varieties? Many official assessments permit only one response, and offer informants little or no room for explanation or qualification. There are of course inherent problems with the whole questionnaire/interview approach, especially when it exists in tightly structured or 'closed' format. However, enquiries that permit more 'open-ended' responding – that allow respondents to elaborate on their multilingual abilities, for instance – lead to further difficulties in accurately assessing what respondents have understood questions to mean and, therefore, in the accurate recording of information. In the 1986 Canadian census, one question was 'can you speak English or French well enough to conduct a conversation?' This is obviously open to a huge degree of interpretation by the informants. Another asked 'what language do you yourself speak at home now (if more than one language, which language do you speak most often)?' Again, problems.

One of the reasons mentioned above for asking about language on censuses is to gauge the effects of formal policies. As with mother-tongue enquiries and those more explicitly focusing upon respondents' current language competence, however, more pointed questions also have attendant problems. In Ireland, where competence in the Irish language declined dramatically in the nineteenth century, 25 per cent of the population reported themselves as Irish speakers in 1861, and this actually rose to 28 per cent in 1971, the highest percentage in a century. By 1991, the figure had increased again, to almost 35 per cent, and the latest census (2006) finds about 41 per cent self-reported speakers of Irish. To interpret these apparently remarkable figures as constituting a substantial upswing in the fortunes of the language would be quite inaccurate, however. While most of the 1861 informants were fluent in Irish, only about 3 per cent of contemporary 'Irish speakers' are. Recent percentages refer in the main to those who have acquired a very thin wash of Irish competence through the schools. More detailed census findings bear this out: the reporting of Irish-speaking ability declines with age, with the highest numbers found among secondary school pupils. As for actual usage, only about one-quarter of the overall 40 per cent who claim Irish-speaking ability say they use the language with any regularity, and three-quarters of *those* are school children.

At one time, there was considerable *under*-reporting of Gaelic competence in Nova Scotia, due largely to the desire to deny possession of a stigmatized variety and to avoid the attentions of 'impertinent, inquisitive and romantic' outsiders. In Ireland, too, it is quite probable that the nineteenth-century enumerations suffered from conscious under-claiming of language ability. Equally, however, we might expect that in modern Ireland *over*-claiming would be more likely. Conscious distortion because of social and political perceptions – whether inaccurate or not, whether reprehensible or not – is a common enough difficulty, after all, when people are asked about sensitive matters (not just linguistic ones).

On a closely related matter, we find that census questions sometimes probe ethnic background instead of, or to complement, questions about language *per se*. In some cases, too, people have been asked about their ethnicity in one census, and about their language in another. Changes here are obviously driven by changing social and political postures and atmospheres, and often reflect heightened inter-group sensitivity. The fact remains, however, that such alterations severely hamper the accurate plotting of information over time, particularly when inferences about language are made on the basis of responses about ethnicity. In the American census of 1980, a possible response to a question about ethnic origins was 'Spanish-Hispanic', a label that could be seen to serve as a unification for all the varied groups that speak Spanish – or who are reputed to, or who would like to, or who want increased funding for Spanish-language education, and so on. 'Ethnic' questions can have an elasticity even greater than that which bedevils the interpretation of language enquiries.

Indians, Chinese and Malays constitute the principal ethnic groups in Singapore and these have served, sometimes in rather clumsy fashion, as recognized language groupings as well. Thus, even though Indians in Singapore may speak Malayalam or Gujerati, officialdom has designated Tamil as 'their' language. Very few Chinese have Mandarin as a true mother tongue (Hokkien, Teochew and Cantonese are the major variants), but it is nevertheless 'theirs', a reflection of government policy to promote Mandarin (and English) and to discourage other Chinese 'dialects'. A few years ago, the Singapore *Straits Times* reported that a civil servant who was ethnically Chinese – but whose mother tongue was Malay, and whose second language was English – was denied permission to sit for an examination in Malay. It was officially considered 'only natural' that he should be competent in his 'designated' mother tongue, Mandarin.

One obvious implication of all these actual and potential confusions is that, when accurate language data are needed, specialized surveys usually must be conducted. These may build upon census information and, in some countries, it is possible to have customized tabulations prepared by central statistical authorities. (Sometimes not, however: in Belgium, *all* language-related questions were abolished in censuses after 1947 because of the possible political, ethnic and social ramifications in that linguistically riven state.) Usually, though, special field work is required. For a comprehensive understanding of non-official languages in Canada (that is, those other than English and French), for example, detailed surveys of ethnic groups in metropolitan areas have been carried out since the 1970s, and similar projects have assessed the 'other languages' of many countries around the world. The scholarly literature is also full of tightly focused studies of particular groups, regions, languages and social settings. In short, census investigations cannot ask about language matters with sufficient scope and breadth to illuminate the details that language planners and policy-makers might really require for accurate assessment and action. Serious enquiries about language may begin by looking at census information, but they must inevitably go well beyond it.

# CHAPTER FIVE

# The Consequences of Babel: Lingua Francas

## The Lingua Franca

A multilingual world means that language divides exist, and we have a number of ways to bridge them beyond individual abilities that, however broad, are obviously very limited in the great scheme of things. The two most common spans are lingua francas and translation. The former fall into three categories. First, there are existing languages that have achieved some position of power, either regionally or globally: these big varieties are sometimes referred to as 'languages of wider communication'. Second, there are restricted or limited forms of existing languages, whose diminished scope is easy to master and sufficient for simple communicative purposes: pidgin and creole varieties are the prime examples here. Less common is the use of constructed or 'artificial' languages that are intended, again, to be easy to learn, and which present themselves as universal auxiliaries that do not threaten mother tongues.

Although there must have been earlier examples, the 'original' lingua franca (that is to say, the 'language of the Franks') was a medium for trade and commerce, dating from the time of the Crusaders' struggles in the eastern Mediterranean. It was probably a pidgin (see below) composed of Provençal – common along the Riviera, from Marseille to Genoa – and Italian, with the latter being the dominant element. The word 'Frank' suggests eastern influence, inasmuch as it is related to *feringhi*, an Arabic word denoting any European (or, sometimes, any Christian). *Lingua franca* was undoubtedly used by the people of the Levant, in a rough-and-ready fashion, to mean any European variety in circumstances in which further specificity was not needed. But it referred, above all, to the mixture that Arabs (and others) heard the 'Franks' of different mother tongues using among themselves, and this was basically a Provençal-Italian mix, although there were probably other linguistic contributors, too. Early uses of the term typically refer to a 'mixed language' or 'jargon'; from this it became generalized to signify any 'contact' language. In the seventeenth century, the poet Dryden thus observed that a lingua franca was a compound language of 'all tongues'; his is apparently the first recorded use of the term in English. By the end of the nineteenth century, the term had expanded to include instances where a single language provided the necessary bridging (e.g. Urdu in India; Swahili in East Africa), but the earlier idea of some mixture of varieties was also retained.

# Languages of Wider Communication

Almost everyone knows that there have always existed important and prestigious languages that served as bridges among national groups and language communities. Many still seem not to know, however, that these languages achieved their power and status because of the social and political dominance of their users and not because of any intrinsic linguistic qualities. The popular and enduring argument has been that some language varieties are inherently better than the others, either on 'logical' (which means 'grammatical') or on aesthetic grounds. While equivalent grammatical 'goodness' across languages was touched upon in the opening chapter, research has also shown that the argument fails at the aesthetic level, too. In one study, Welsh adults who knew no French were presented with several varieties of that language and asked to evaluate the pleasantness (and 'prestige', too) of the voices. No regular patterns emerged, even though French speakers themselves clearly preferred European French over working-class Quebec French. In another experiment, British undergraduates who knew no Greek evaluated the aesthetic quality of two Greek dialects, the Athenian and the Cretan. The former is the prestige standard form, while the latter is a non-standard variant of low social status; within the Greek speech community, the language of the capital is heard as more mellifluous, while the island variety is considered rougher in quality. As in the first investigation, however, the listener-judges were able to detect no uniform differences between the two dialects.

The compelling element in these demonstrations is the judges' ignorance of the social connotations that the different varieties clearly possess in their own speech communities. The implication is that, if one removes (experimentally) the social stereotypes usually associated with given varieties, aesthetic judgements favouring the high-status dialects will not arise. Of course, none of this rules out purely individual preferences: I may think Italian sounds the most attractive, while Gaelic may fall most sweetly on your ear, but we should agree to differ on a matter of subjectivity that seems to admit of no general yardstick.

Powerful languages are dominant, then, because of the military, political, social and economic might of their speakers. There are examples in which a more purely cultural status supports the lingua franca function that rests upon dominance. This status has, however, generally grown from earlier associations with those more blatant elements just mentioned. In any case, the strength of lingua francas arises from the fact that their original users possess important commodities – wealth, imperial dominance, cultural superiority, scientific and technical knowledge – that others see as desirable or necessary for their own aspirations. The aphorism that 'all roads lead to Rome' has always had linguistic and cultural meaning, too.

I have already said that Greek and Latin were classical lingua francas. By the fourth century BC, Greek had spread throughout the near and middle East. The Romans, more ardent imperialists, ensured that Latin had a still greater sway. Indeed, even after the emergence of the romance varieties that it spawned, Latin remained as an instrument of religion and scholarship, weakening only with the rise of secularism, mercantilism and the 'new science'. The last major English philosophical work to be published in Latin was Bacon's *Novum Organum* (in 1623), and the last important scientific work was Newton's *Philosophiae Naturalis Principia Mathematica* (in 1687). After Latin, several other European languages took their turn in the (western) sun: French and Italian are particularly notable here. Today, of course, English is the most important global variety and thus has the greatest status as a world lingua franca (see also Chapter 8).

## Pidgins and Creoles

The second major type of lingua franca is that of a restricted or simplified language mixture; indeed, as noted above, the very term *lingua franca* first had this connotation exclusively. Such a mixture is referred to as a *pidgin*, a word whose etymology is unclear. In his *Voyage to China*, published in 1850, Julius Berncastle wrote that:

> The Chinese not being able to pronounce the word 'business', called it 'bigeon', which has degenerated into 'pigeon', so that this word is in constant use.

Another possibility is that pidgin derives from *pigeon* (a bird that can carry simple messages; perhaps there is also some sense here of the bird-like and rather superficial repetitions associated with trade communication). Whatever the derivation, pidgin refers to a mixture of languages that is no one's maternal variety, a spartan and purely instrumental medium.

There are many pidgins in use, most involving a European colonial language. Their restricted vocabulary and grammar allow simple communication and, since this is their purpose, the very existence of pidgins does suggest some linguistic creativity. Although some pidgins have considerable longevity, many do not last long: if the communities in contact (trading settlements and indigenous populations, for example) drift apart, then clearly the pidgin is no longer needed. In other cases, where prolonged contact exists, one group may learn the other's language. In the linguistically diverse Papua New Guinea, *Tok Pisin* ('talk pidgin', New Guinea Pidgin) is in fact officially recognized, and is the most important 'native' variety, spoken by several million people on a regular basis. Here are the opening lines of the Lord's Prayer in Tok Pisin:

Papa bilong mipela
Yu stap long heven.
Nem bilong yu i mas i stap holi.
Kingdom bilong yu i mas i kam.

Closely related to pidgins are *koinēs*. These also involve mixing and linguistic simplification but, unlike pidgins, are derived from varieties that are either mutually intelligible or, at least, similar. 'Koinē' simply means 'common language' (in Greek) and, like all lingua francas, it does not replace existing varieties: it is not to be confused, then, with more phoenix-like forms. 'Koinēization' is a more gradual process than 'pidginization', requiring sustained contact and, indeed, integration. The term was first applied to the type of Greek that became an eastern Mediterranean lingua franca; this was essentially Attic Greek with intertwined elements from other dialects. New Zealand English and Quebec French are contemporary koinēs.

A pidgin may evolve into a *creole*. This happens when a pidgin becomes a mother tongue, when children born in pidgin-speaking communities begin to develop (or 'creolize') their linguistic inheritance. The developing language becomes richer, more expressive and more linguistically complete than the parent variety. Nobody's mother tongue becomes somebody's mother tongue. As Peter Trudgill has put it, the simplifications and reductions that characterize pidgins are 'repaired by expansion'; they are 'perfectly normal languages – only their history is somewhat unusual'. *Creole* itself is generally thought to derive from the Portuguese *crioulo*, via the French *créole*. It meant a person of European descent who was born and reared in a colonial setting. The meaning gradually shifted to include Africans born in the (non-African) colonies and, further, to encompass the social and linguistic practices of such creole persons. Now, in its linguistic sense at least, 'creole' means an expanded pidgin.

A national language of Sierra Leone is Krio (creole); it arose from an English-African (especially Yoruba) pidgin, is the maternal variety of perhaps 10 per cent of the population, and is understood by almost everyone in the country (i.e. by about six million people). 'A bin tek di buk go na skul' ('I took the book to school') and 'I don was di klos' ('He has washed the clothes') are examples. In combination with other languages, Krio now spawns pidgin varieties itself, thus giving us a glimpse of the ever-evolving and dynamic state of language development.

## Constructed Languages

'Artificial' or constructed languages – supporters now view the former designation disapprovingly – are the third type of lingua franca. The example most readers will know is Esperanto, presented to the world by Ludwig Zamenhof in 1887. For many, both within and without academia, the whole idea of constructed languages immediately suggests a sort of linguistic lunatic fringe or, at best, profoundly misguided enthusiasm. Esperanto and other languages like it are seen as the fantasy creations of eccentrics and cranks. Nonetheless, the interest in constructed languages is an outgrowth of that early and pervasive quest for the first human language, the language of Eden, that I discussed in the opening chapter.

The next part of the story of a 'perfect' – or, at least, more perfect – language moves on from the notion of some 'Adamic' *lingua humana* to the construction of a 'universal' or 'philosophical' language, whose logic must inevitably facilitate the search for knowledge and its classification. Not surprisingly, then, the same age that saw the dawn of the 'new science' in Europe also saw great activity on the part of the 'language projectors'. Indeed, most of the early members of the Royal Society were at least passively interested in the idea of a 'philosophical' medium. As well, continental luminaries like Comenius, Descartes and Leibniz were all interested in a universal auxiliary language that could cross group boundaries and that would assist in the evolution of the new Baconian science.

While 'philosophical' language projects came to naught, the desire for neutrality – for a medium that, while logical and regular, privileges no one particular group of speakers – remained. Powerful 'natural' languages cannot serve here (at least, not in the eyes of the language makers) for they are tinged, as it were, by history and (usually) imperialism. Thus, the way has been seen as theoretically clear for a constructed language to fill a yawning and bothersome gap. Since the seventeenth century, there have been hundreds of universal-language schemes. Although the rhetoric surrounding constructed languages has often been very grandiose indeed, they have all swung on two pivots: a practical instrumentality, on the one hand, and a naïve but laudable desire to facilitate global harmony, on the other. Thus Zamenhof felt that Esperanto would provide more than a universal second language to supplement, but not supplant, mother tongues. He hoped and believed that it could also contribute greatly to some 'trans-national identity', an apt goal for one who observed that 'if the nationalism of the strong is ignoble, the nationalism of the weak is imprudent'. To dilute the former while resisting the latter must have seemed a pressing need when Zamenhof said this – in 1914.

Zamenhof's Esperanto, while not the last word in constructed languages, is certainly the most successful. There *may* be as many as two million Esperanto speakers worldwide, but the fact that official estimates give that as an upper possible limit, and 100,000 as a lower, suggests the dubious state of statistics here. There are also some native speakers, children whose parents have brought them up with Esperanto as a first language; again, estimates vary widely, from perhaps as many as 2,000 to perhaps as few as 200. The core of Esperanto is its famous sixteen-rule grammar, and its guiding force is simplicity and regularity: all nouns end in *o*, the definite article *la* serves for all cases, numbers and sexes, verb forms are the same regardless of person or number, the stress is always on the penultimate syllable, and so forth.

Foremost among constructed languages though it is, Esperanto has never captured a sufficient amount of general attention to become the functioning worldwide auxiliary its proponents wish. One rough distinction seems to be between those who, while not wholly unsympathetic to the idea of constructed languages, nevertheless perceive fatal practical flaws, and those who see Esperantists (and other constructed-language apologists) more or less as cranks and faddists. It is not unfair to say that all constructed languages have suffered from suspicions of naïve idealism, lack of intellectual rigour and even presumption (how can you invent a language?). At a pragmatic level, the apparently reasonable desire to have everyone learn the same link language founders on a logical reef. Since the speech community within which Esperanto (say) could be used is very restricted and its members widely scattered, it is hard to recruit substantial numbers of new learners. But how will a meaningful community ever arise unless recruitment happens? Motivating people to take the plunge has always been the central difficulty dogging proponents of constructed languages. This is particularly so in societies in which powerful languages already hold sway, and still more so when these other languages are, like English, contenders for global lingua franca status.

The attention I have given to constructed languages here does not reflect any personal adherence or activism. It is simply that this type of lingua franca seems to represent a logical and 'neutral' solution to communication problems, but is both little and inaccurately known, both within and without academia. Sociolinguists, for instance, have largely neglected, prejudged or seen as taboo the whole area even though, as one writer put it, there are 'facts, texts, and living subjects readily available' for study. While a few scholars have interested themselves in constructed languages, these interests have rarely translated into research. The little formal study that does exist has been largely of the opinion-poll variety, and has not generally shown much rigour in either sampling or analysis. Apart from language study *per se*, the important connections between language and identity should also prompt investigation of the psychology, politics and sociology of constructed-language activism. Socio-religious investigation suggests itself, too, for there has frequently been a quasi-religious element to such activism: Zamenhof revealed this in his later years, for instance, and Esperantists have often rejected other constructed-language adherents as heretics from the true cause, sometimes quite vitriolically. George Orwell once wrote that 'for sheer dirtiness of fighting, the feud between the inventors of various of the international languages would take a lot of beating'.

# CHAPTER SIX

# The Consequences of Babel: Translation

## Translation, Ownership and Secrecy

While the previous chapter dealt with different types of lingua francas, a second broad approach to bridging language gaps is that of translation. While translation is of obvious practical use, it has sometimes been seen to have unfavourable social and psychological consequences. Since these are not always well understood, it is appropriate to begin with a brief examination of some of them.

The translator is one whose linguistic competence gives entry to (at least) two language communities and, as George Steiner has pointed out, 'there is in every act of translation – and specially where it succeeds – a touch of treason. Hoarded dreams, patents of life are being taken across the frontier'. The old Italian proverb is blunter: *traduttori, traditori*. And what are these dreams, these patents of life, if not the cultural heart of the community? Concealment and privacy, as many scholars have pointed out, are as much features of language as is communication: Karl Popper, for instance, wrote that 'what is most characteristic of the human language is the possibility of story telling'. This is but a recent expression of a very old idea, all examples of which refer to that aspect of language that Steiner called 'enclosure and willed opaqueness'.

The idea, indeed, often assumes deep religious significance. The Buddhist Sutras, the Hindu Vedas, the Christian Bible, the Holy Qu'ran and the Hadith, the Torah and the Talmud, and many other religious works are all sacred in and of themselves, to varying degrees. Some, for instance, are not to be translated at all, while particular versions of others (the King James Bible, for example) have achieved iconic status. The idea of the holiness of 'the word' – of a linkage between words and things, of divine creation, even of the creator itself – predates both the Christian era and the Greek Golden Age. Some time during the twenty-fifth Egyptian dynasty (that is, between about 750 and 650 BC), an already existing theological discussion was inscribed on a stone, now in the British Museum. In this 'Memphite Theology', we read that the god Ptah, having first *thought* the world, then *created* it by saying the name of all its elements. Thus, in the Egyptian mythology, as in later ones, names and things coincided, the former perfectly capturing the essence of the latter. In the Christian tradition, too, there is the mystical association of the 'word' – *logos*, the Greek λόγος, with its many related meanings of word, thought, essential principle, reason and logic – with the all-pervasive and divine spirit. We read this at the opening of St John's gospel in the most forthright way:

> In the beginning was the Word, and the Word was with God, and the Word was God ... and the Word was made flesh, and dwelt among us.

It follows that any tampering with the Word is of the utmost gravity. Indeed, there are clear demonstrations – in Judaism and Christianity, to give but two examples – that translation is blasphemy. He who has 'been in Christ' must not (or, perhaps, cannot) repeat the *arcana verba* in mortal words (II *Corinthians* XII: 4). And Jewish writings from the first century record the belief that the translation of the holy law into Greek led to three days of darkness. There are groups who believe that the name of God is never to be uttered, others who reserve this honour for the priestly caste and still others who argue that *no* language at all is adequate for religious purposes.

# Voice Appropriation

Privacy, the construction of fictionalized myths, legends and stories – to say nothing of outright dissimulation – are at once important and threatened by translation and translators. A modern expression of these age-old concerns for the protection of identity, and for the potential erosion of that protection by translation, is the alleged 'appropriation' of native stories by outsiders. In many cultures, particularly those with powerful and rich oral traditions, stories *belong* to the group or, indeed, to some designated story-teller or caste of story-tellers. Consider the role of the European bards, the *shamans* of North America or the *griots* of West Africa: living libraries, charged with the preservation and transmission of the most central and important group narratives.

The phenomenon of 'voice appropriation' arises from two related resentments felt by many communities. The first, as we have seen, is that the very names by which they are most widely known are not of their own choosing. The second is that important myths and legends have often been told by outsiders. This cultural theft is generally seen as a continuation of colonialism. 'Insiders' have always disliked and feared intrusion into the heart of their society, of course – think what it means to have large and powerful neighbours give you the name by which the wider world will know you, tell your stories, reveal your secrets. It is only recently, however, that this resentment has been acknowledged and accepted by 'outsiders', a reflection of shifts of attitude on the one hand and of greater self-assertiveness on the other. That is, the political clout of small speech communities, and the (apparently) greater willingness of larger ones to listen, support and respond, has never been as evident as it is today. Of course, there remains much 'mainstream' hypocrisy, empty posturing and repellent lip-service, but there has been substantive change, too, at least in western liberal democracies. The 'indigenous voice' – to cite the title of an important collection published some twenty years ago – has never been so united and forceful in its repudiation of what might be seen as a type of 'linguistic imperialism'.

There are examples here from around the globe. Studies of the fortunes of Scottish Gaelic, for example, have shown that the voices of 'in-group' members have not been sufficiently heard. A common explanation is that 'ordinary' people have been unable or unwilling to record their own perspectives on important events, but this does not come to grips with the overwhelming English historiographical bias. There *are* Gaelic commentaries available, but they have been largely ignored by historians. The generality here is surely as a corollary of the familiar dictum that history is written by the winners. An important implication recalls the often pejorative naming practices that I discussed earlier: if outsiders who have been traditionally considered as inferior or alien have come to achieve obvious social and political dominance, what does this suggest to the 'insiders' about the validity of their traditional descriptions, about their self-esteem, about the tenuous nature of their cultural continuity?

Nonetheless, I think that we have to be careful when discussing 'appropriation' because, no matter how much one may sympathize with individuals and cultures who have been badly treated by more powerful societies, the matter is by no means clear-cut. In works of fiction, for instance, 'appropriation' of one sort or another is paramount. A logical extension of the appropriation argument might lead to the conclusion that no one could ever write about anything beyond one's own immediate experience; only 'insiders' could write about their lives and cultures. Consider, too, that an embargo along these lines, one that would prevent majority-group outsiders from writing about the lives of those in small or culturally threatened groups, would logically also prevent minority-group members from commenting upon the 'mainstream'. Furthermore: are women never to write about men, blacks never about whites, Germans never about Spaniards? This is clearly nonsensical, an imposition that would have stifled an overwhelmingly huge proportion of the world's literature, and of the knowledge we have of one another as human beings.

At the same time, it is not difficult to understand the grievances that arise when the narrative boundaries that are crossed separate groups of significantly different socioeconomic clout. Sauce for the goose may, logically, be sauce for the gander, but the inequalities that exist between those birds in real life surely mean that some special attention might reasonably be given to the less powerful ones. Dostoevsky famously said that we could judge the state of a civilization by seeing how it runs its prisons, and many others have enlarged the point: the way society treats its most needy or vulnerable citizens is a measure of its humanity. And we can surely expand things further still, and say that there must also be a correlation between that humanity and cross-cultural sensitivity. This is why the more thoughtful commentaries on 'voice appropriation' have not stated matters in a simplistic either-or fashion but, rather, have argued about the *degree* of cross-border commentary that might be reasonable, and the circumstances and contexts in which it ought or ought not to occur.

# Translation in Practice

Putting aside these negative features of translation and its ramifications, we can turn to more mundane aspects. Translation is simply a fact of multilingual life, but it is not, however, a simple or technical one. Apart from almost useless word-for-word exercises, every act of translation involves interpretation and judgement. For this reason, it has sometimes been supposed that 'true' translation is impossible. However, although a perfect version which captures *every* nuance and allusion is rather unlikely – and becomes more so as the material to be translated becomes less prosaic – we have nonetheless translated, for practical purposes, throughout history. To turn again to George Steiner:

> to dismiss the validity of translation because it is not always possible and never perfect is absurd ... the defence of translation has the immense advantage of abundant, vulgar fact.

To understand translation as interpretation also links, incidentally, cross-language exercises with communications within the same language. That is, even the simplest of conversations between two speakers of the same language involves interpretation, and is analogous to 'reading between the lines' in written language. And it is in the written language of the past that the case becomes clearest: even the work of Charles Dickens now begins to look a bit alien to many, and the works of Chaucer are regularly presented in what amount to bilingual editions. It is through a constant process of translation that we continue to possess our own literature and, indeed, our own culture.

From the time of Cicero's admonition not simply to translate *verbum pro verbo*, we have been faced with the practical problems of the translation exercise. Dryden's observation when translating Virgil into English (in 1697) is illustrative here. 'I thought fit,' he wrote, 'to steer betwixt the two extremes of paraphrase and literal translation ... I have endeavoured to make Virgil speak such English as he would himself have spoken, if he had been born in England, and in this present age'. This most basic of concerns has not faded away over the last two centuries; in fact, it remains the most immediately pressing for the day-to-day enterprise of the translator. Émile Rieu (an editor of Zola's books in

English translation) here referred to what he called the 'law of equivalent effect'. Since, for example, *Germinal* is a violent and emotional book about strife between owners and workers in northern French collieries, any translation which cast the dialogue in 'refined' or more polite language would have been ludicrous, and a travesty of Zola's intent. When translating *L'Assommoir*, Leonard Tancock kept Rieu's admonition firmly in mind; the book, he noted

> is for Paris what a rich novel of Cockney life would
> be for London ... the nicknames Bec-Salé, Bibi-la-Grillade,
> Mes Bottes, Gueule d'or ... have as authentic a ring as,
> say, Nobby Clark or Ally Sloper or for that matter
> Fanny Adams might have to a Londoner.

Problems here can be formidable. 'The translation of slang and swearing in general', Tancock continued, 'is self-defeating in that the more exactly it hits off the tone of the original in the slang of the moment ... the less durable it is likely to be'. The only solution is re-translation. Thus, new versions of the classics have always been seen as vital to their continued popular existence.

I find it interesting that the greatest threats to accurate translation appear at opposite ends of the literary continuum. On one hand, rough and slang-laden speech poses the sorts of difficulties Tancock discusses; on the other, poetic or philosophical productions also lay traps in their use of metaphor, allusion or dense, abstract reasoning. Taken all in all, the difficulties faced by translators have remained remarkably stable, from Cicero's day to our own. Does a literal version or a more literary one come first? Should translations aim largely to recreate the linguistic world of the original, or should they try and bring things up to date? How much freedom should the translator exercise? These are some of the fundamental concerns of all translation exercises. Most readers may be inclined to side with Cicero – and Rieu – but they should also be aware that Vladimir Nabokov once argued that anything but the 'clumsiest literalism' is fraudulent in the translation of poetry. What *can* he have meant?

It is of course obvious that some words, and some works, are easier to translate than others. Poetry, as I say, is more difficult than prose. And, within prose, Agatha Christie is probably easier than James Joyce. However, even an author as apparently prosaic as the creator of Hercule Poirot can create difficulties for the translator. Josef Škvorecký writes that, in Czech translation, Christie's clever Belgian detective is made to sound more like the other characters than he is in Christie's original, where his English is considerably 'Frenchified'. (David Suchet's television interpretation of Poirot is very accurate in this regard.) The result, Škvorecký tells us, is that Poirot makes Czech readers think of a Sudeten German. More interesting still are the efforts to translate Christie into French, to render Poirot's Frenchified English into French itself. In the original, Christie has Poirot say:

> Stamboul, it is a city I have never visited. It would be a pity to pass through *comme ça* [he snaps his fingers]. Nothing presses – I shall remain there as a tourist for a few days.

In Postif's translation for the *Librairie des Champs-Elysées*, this is rendered as 'ne connaissant pas Stamboul, je ne voudrai pas y passer sans m'arrêter. Rien ne me presse. Je visiterai la ville en touriste'. Not quite the *même chose*, is it?

# CHAPTER SEVEN

# Keeping Languages Pure

## Purism and Prescriptivism

A world of languages, as I have implied throughout this book, is also a world of identities, and many linguistic attitudes and actions are therefore reflections of underlying psychological and social matters having to do, above all, with ethnic and national memberships and allegiances. Once a strong relationship has been established between a particular language and a particular group affiliation, the 'protection' of the language often becomes paramount. This generally takes the form of purist and prescriptivist impulses and actions to keep a language undefiled by unwanted linguistic intrusions; these are typically part and parcel of prescriptivist regulations about what is linguistically 'correct' or not. All such activities ostensibly deal with language *per se*, but they are essentially in the service of *identity* protection.

In a theoretical treatment of linguistic purism, George Thomas made some general points that we can use here to anchor our discussion. He noted, first, that attempts at purism and prescriptivism are universal characteristics of standardized (and standardizing) languages; second, that the forms these attempts take are often remarkably similar across contexts; third, that while prescriptivist actions are usually directed at unwanted external influences, internal prescriptivism (selecting among dialects, for instance) is also common; fourth, that most such activity is concerned with vocabulary items, although grammatical regulation is often an important component of internal prescriptivism. Language practices and planning exist in a circular relationship with the desires that motivate them: if our cultural impulses have linguistic consequences, then these, in turn, will influence our thoughts on social identity and social categorization.

The clearest examples of language protection are found in the existence and the works of academies. The most well-known of these is the *Académie française*. Here, Cardinal Richelieu's forty 'immortals' were given virtually absolute power to prescribe in literary and linguistic matters. As we shall see, the efforts of the French academy and other similar institutions have not always been very successful, either in their grammatical and lexicographical productions or, more specifically, in their attempts to intervene in the dynamics of language use. But this does not detract from their importance as manifestations of will and intent, nor does it vitiate their symbolic role. In fact, while lack of success here may tell us quite a lot about the power of language to resist institutionalized direction, the very establishment of language academies and councils – and their continued existence in spite of poor track records – tells us even more about the importance of language as a marker of group identity. Formal pronouncements on language matters continue to mark linguistic and nationalistic anxieties and these, whatever the logic of the matter, persist in the popular imagination. We may be sure that, when Maurice Druon – a former Minister of Culture and the *secrétaire perpétuel* of the *Académie française* – called for language watchdogs to guard against poor French on television, a great many people nodded in agreement.

The letters pages of newspapers everywhere regularly print feverish responses to linguistic barbarisms and bastardizations, there have always been influential columnists who write about usage and abusage, and books about the decline of the language and what ought to be done to stem it are both frequent and popular. There has never been a shortage of 'amateur do-gooding missionaries' in this perennially interesting area, as Sir Randolph Quirk once observed. All such evangelical zeal can be easily derided, and, furthermore, there is often a dark side arising from prejudice and ignorance. Some of the criticism, however, is more reasoned, particularly that which deals with deliberate or ignorant misuse of existing words, propaganda, jargon and unnecessary neologism. Here we often find literary critics – not linguists, perhaps, but not rank amateurs either – adding their voices to the debate. One thinks immediately, I suppose, of Orwell's famous essays on the status of English and the politics of language, but there are many other thoughtful treatments here. Running through all such efforts, whether careful or ill-conceived, is a concern for language, and it is not always an ignoble one.

In modern times, prescriptivism has not been very popular among linguists, who have typically held it to be neither desirable nor feasible to attempt to intervene in the social life of language. A deliberate renunciation of prescriptivism, of course, is more like atheism than agnosticism: a conscious non-belief is, after all, a belief itself, and scholarly stances against language intervention represent a sort of 'reverse purism'. It has been suggested that, in their rush away from prescriptivism, linguists may have abdicated a useful role as arbiters, and may have left much of the field open to those less well-informed. The late Dwight Bolinger was one of the few contemporary linguists willing to participate in debates about the 'public life' of language: he rightly criticized the obvious crank elements, but he also understood the desire for standards, the popular frustration with perceived 'decay' and 'incorrectness', the onslaught of jargon. In my view, there remains a need for much more illumination of that persistent no-man's-land between academic linguistics and public language.

Prescriptivist attitudes towards language have always been with us, and complaints about decline and decay, about foreign infiltration and about the inadequacy of certain varieties are as perennial as misgivings about the younger generation. Within the scholarly community, there is a long tradition of studying language attitudes, supplemented more recently by a revived interest in 'folk linguistics', in popular understandings of language, its use and its users. This sort of attention has traditionally coincided with arguments against prescriptivist intervention, on the grounds already noted. Historically, of course, matters were rather different in intellectual and policy circles: decisions have been required when national languages arose and became elements in group identity, when some print standardization was found necessary, when popular literacy grew. Interventions here did not simply emerge from the minds of some nationalist élite aiming to forge or strengthen group solidarity.

The tension between a prescriptivism arising from narrow and often unfair conceptions of social inclusion and exclusion, and desires and needs for at least *some* standardization remains important today. Any attention to the work of 'language planners' immediately reveals prescriptivist stances. Any desire to intervene on behalf of beleaguered varieties (for example), a desire that has become attractive to many, both within and without the academy, involves a willingness to engage in prescriptivist exercises. This can create an interesting conundrum, to be sure, for those whose liberal impulses generally embrace *both* a concern for the small, the 'authentic' and the 'threatened' *and* a dislike of 'interfering' in other cultures. I shall return to the topic of endangered languages in the concluding chapters here.

As I noted at the beginning, a strong connection between nationalism and language leads very naturally to desires to 'protect' and perhaps 'purify' that language. Of course, the notion of keeping a language free from foreign taint reveals a profound misunderstanding of the unfettered dynamics of all natural languages, but it also reveals a great deal about psychological and social perceptions. It is simply a fact of social life that, as Quirk observed, 'protagonists of national languages tend to involve themselves with questions of linguistic purity.' Indeed, as my brief reference to the demands of printing reveals, interest in linguistic protection and preservation predates the modern wave of nationalism by at least a century or so. This in turn reflects an earlier historical wave, one in which the power of Latin waned and that of the major European languages began to wax: as the latter began to flex their muscles, they naturally felt the need for standardization of various sorts. And there were identity functions to be served from the beginning, too, even if they were initially more focused upon the unification of the literate than upon a broader nationalistic 'groupness'. It is certainly possible, however, to see the early efforts as providing an important base for the nationalist impulses that were to come.

# Academies

The beginning of institutionalized purism came with the establishment of the *Accademia della Crusca* in Florence in 1582. It was, however, the *Académie française* (founded 1635) that set the pattern for many of the similarly inclined bodies that were to follow in Europe and beyond. Its major aim was to reinforce its conceptions of linguistic clarity, simplicity and good taste, to encourage all that was 'noble, polished and reasonable'. Most academicians were initially drawn from the church, the nobility or the top echelons of the army, the bodies that would naturally have been considered the inheritors of the best French and the obvious arbiters of good linguistic taste. From the beginning, professional linguists have rarely been members. Since the notion of language purity is a fiction anyway, perhaps there is no pressing requirement for 'experts'. Intelligent, educated individuals from the professions, the literary world and politics are all reasonable people to have as members, falling as they do between linguists and philologists, on the one hand, and the man or woman in the street – whose beliefs comprise that 'folk' linguistics mentioned above – on the other. However, since dictionary-making and the production of grammars *do* require specialist skills, it will come as no surprise to learn that the academy's first effort here (in 1694) was the inferior piece of work that might be expected from an amateur, if socially prominent, collective.

In modern times, the *Académie française* has become best known for its attempts to keep French free of foreign borrowings and to create, where necessary, French terms for the products and processes of science and technology. It has thus acquired a modernizing function to supplement the original purifying objective. The special aim of keeping *English* influence at bay began in the nineteenth century and has strengthened since then. Purification plus gate-keeping: these are obvious undertakings on behalf of the maintenance of group boundaries and identity.

Similar in intent to the French academy, and much influenced by it, was the *Real Academia Española*, founded in 1713 by the Bourbon king Philip V. Its royal motto – *Limpia, fija y da esplendor* – emphasizes again the desire for linguistic purification. A dictionary was produced in 1730 and a grammar in 1771. Much of the importance of the academy rests upon the way in which it spread its influence to the Spanish New World, spawning a large number of associated bodies in the nineteenth century. Their common brief has been to work for the unity of Spanish and to enshrine historically based standards. It is important to understand that these are not merely the aspirations of language dilettantes or popular commentators; rather, they reflect the views of Spanish linguists. As Quirk (again) has pointed out, there is an interesting difference in national attitudes between these Hispanic professionals and their counterparts in the English-speaking world, where national academies have not been generally supported (see below).

Academies charged with maintaining linguistic standards exist far beyond the Romance area and, in countries lacking a formal academy, councils and other prescriptive bodies typically exist (as with the agencies charged with the promotion of Swahili in Kenya and Tanzania, for example). As William Mackey wrote, 'there is hardly any country in the world that does not have some sort of public or private language planning body'. Conspicuous by its absence, however, is an English-language academy; neither England nor America established one, and this anglophone anomaly extends to all the relevant overseas countries as well – with the exception of the English Academy of Southern Africa, established in 1961, and the 'academy' of the Queen's English Society (see below); both, however, are non-governmental organizations.

Quirk (once more) suggested that there must exist some Anglo-Saxon aversion to 'linguistic engineering', or a lack of interest in formal activities to maintain linguistic standards. Others agree, arguing further that this is a luxury available only to those whose language has become so globally dominant. But the point of view is a historically limited one. Consider the position of English in the late sixteenth century: very few people then would have predicted global status for a language that had only four or five million speakers and, more importantly, one that was ranked well behind its counterparts. Indeed, there was then a flourishing trade in books aimed at English travellers to the continent. John Florio, for example, published his *First Fruits* in 1578, a textbook and manual for the teaching of Italian to English gentlemen. French, Spanish and, especially, Italian were the powerful 'languages of wider communication', and English was of little use in this regard once you crossed the Channel. In Tudor and Stuart England, then, second-language learning was a necessity among the educated and commercial classes. Even Queen Elizabeth was a student of Italian.

There have always been proponents of an English academy. Richard Verstegan, who argued for the protection and encouragement of the language in his *Restitution of Decayed Intelligence* (1605), issued an early call for such a body. In 1664, the Royal Society established a committee to 'improve' English, and its members included such luminaries as Dryden, Evelyn and Waller. This might have become the cornerstone of a language academy, but the broad scientific aims of the Royal Society tended to isolate those who were more narrowly concerned with language, and their base of operations soon diminished. (One can reasonably argue, of course, that if there had been a greater degree of interest in English prescriptivism, the initial efforts would not have faded. Dryden and his colleagues must not have been *that* interested, after all.) A little later, Daniel Defoe proposed that England should follow the example of the *Académie française* and establish a body to encourage 'polite' usage, to maintain 'propriety of style' and to purge the unfortunate and irregular additions that 'ignorance and affectation have introduced'. Jonathan Swift, too, argued for an English academy to counter the 'infusion of enthusiastic jargon' that had come to infect the language. None of these schemes and proposals received sufficient or sustained support.

It must not be thought, by the way, that interest in an English academy has disappeared completely. In 2010, the *Economist* reported that the Queen's English Society (established in 1972) had just created a new English Academy in order to combat the current 'anything goes' attitude. The website of the Society itself provides more information about its academy, acknowledges a prescriptivist intent – here, it makes the reasonable point that the organization would have no purpose if it were wholly 'descriptive' – but denies a policing or governing role. It notes that 'the fact, nevertheless, remains that there are people who speak [English] and write it in a clear and elegant way and others who are imprecise and unclear'. The website adds that 'anyone who knows the rules and can use English correctly is entitled to "play" with the language ... [but] there is all the difference between such a person saying "If it ain't broke, don't fix it" and a person who says that believing it to be correct English'. These citations illustrate very well the contemporary face of prescriptivism: a reluctance to be branded authoritative which is nevertheless coupled with strong views about 'correctness'.

# Dictionaries

Even Anglo-Saxons, of course, felt the need of some language standardization, of some arbiter of 'correct' vocabulary and usage. And so, in both Britain and the United States, the production of dictionaries by individuals took the place of the institutional prescriptivist approach commonly found elsewhere. From the middle of the seventeenth century, English lexicographers knew all about the work of the French and Italian academies. Samuel Johnson, who published his famous dictionary in 1755 – often seen, not least by himself, as the English equivalent of the committee efforts of the continental academies – acknowledged them quite specifically. His sense of the functions and force of lexicography altered somewhat over time. In his *Plan of a Dictionary* (1747), he implied both the possibility and the desirability of some degree of prescriptivism. In the preface to the great work itself, however, he criticized the lexicographer who imagines

> that his dictionary can embalm his language, and secure it from corruption and decay, that it is in his power to change sublunary nature, or clear the world at once from folly, vanity and affectation.

Elsewhere in that same preface, Johnson expressed the hope that the 'spirit of English liberty' would hamper or ruin any academy that, after all, came to be established. Nonetheless, he continued to feel that a dictionary resting upon the English of prominent authors might stabilize the language and check its 'degeneration'. Perhaps the clearest statement of Johnson's ambivalence is found in a single sentence: 'the pen must at length comply with the tongue; illiterate writers will ... rise into renown, who, not knowing the original import of words, will use them with colloquial licentiousness, confound distinction, and forget propriety'. Usage *will* have its way, even though lexicographers might wish that a little restraint, a little more 'propriety', might be possible.

Johnson's ambivalence represents very well a more general English posture: on the one hand, the idea of some élite body imposing their will on the language was distasteful; on the other, the need for some guidelines was perfectly obvious, in an era when spelling and usage were fluid, and when language was seen as a potential servant in the cause of identity. This tension between a prescriptivism arising from narrow and often unfair conceptions of social inclusion and exclusion, and desires and needs for at least *some* standardization is, I believe, a permanent one, and it is not restricted to anglophone settings. In fact, a more or less permanent ambivalence or tension is highly desirable. On the one hand, the steadily growing scholarly belief in the 'naturalness' of descriptivism is legitimately erected on the foundations of 'ordinary' usage. *Usus est magister optimus* may be logically unprovable, but it has the considerable weight of history behind it, not least exemplified by language change and evolution. On the other, linguistic choices continue to be necessary, and any route followed means another road not taken. There is, then, an ongoing need for what we might style a 'modified' prescriptivism, for minimalist intervention.

When the United States became independent in 1776, it inherited English linguistic tendencies. In considering language policy, then, it had no academy to consult directly and the Spanish and French models lacked appeal because of their association with 'crowned heads and royal courts'. As in England, some important people *did* favour the idea of an academy, and the most prominent of these was John Adams. He believed that an American academy would restrain the 'natural tendency' that languages had to 'degenerate'. He also believed that, since England had no academy, there was an opportunity here for the United States to put *its* official stamp on linguistic purity and preservation. But Adams, often suspected of monarchist sympathies, had no success in moving Congress. So the result was, once again, recourse to a one-man academy, a lexicographer. The American Johnson was, of course, Noah Webster – who, while acknowledging the need for some uniformities, shared both Johnson's pragmatic perspective on linguistic change and his modesty about the work of dictionary makers.

Webster had more overtly political interests than did Johnson. He felt the need to contribute to the linguistic independence of the United States, a need that culminated in his *American Dictionary of the English Language*, published in 1827. He thought that England and the United States would gradually become linguistically separate, and that entirely different languages would be the eventual result. He was not at all opposed to such a trend, for it reinforced his nationalistic feelings: he *wanted* 'American' to diverge from English. In publications earlier than his great dictionary, Webster had urged spelling changes, and these were to signal the chief differences between American and British English (differences that persist today: *color* rather than *colour*; *center* instead of *centre*). His view was one that I have implied here already: 'a national language is a bond of national union.' Still, enamoured as he was of a new 'people's language', Webster did not shirk from the removal of 'improprieties and vulgarisms ... and ... those odious distinctions of provincial dialects'. Old ideas die hard, even in new countries.

# CHAPTER EIGHT

# Languages and Identities in Transition

## Languages in Contact

One would surely have to be an ostrich not to realize that the 'politics of identity' is particularly prominent these days. Our age is one of transition and transitions are, almost by definition, painful. The break-up of the Soviet Union and consequent re-alignments in eastern Europe, the march of federalism in western Europe, the continuing problems of sub-Saharan Africa, the revolutionary upheavals along the 'Arab street', the emergence of the Asian-Pacific economies, the rethinking of pluralism and multiculturalism in new-world 'receiving' countries (like Canada, Australia and the United States), the struggles of indigenous people in many settings – all these are in flux. And with political negotiation comes linguistic dynamism.

A century ago, Ferdinand de Saussure wrote about the contrasting principles of *provincialism* and *intercourse*, anchor-points whose relevance extends beyond linguistics alone. On the one hand, he argued, provincialism (*l'esprit de clocher*) keeps a community faithful to its traditions and encourages cultural continuity; of course, it also keeps people relatively immobile. On the other, there is an opposing force in the service of broader communication, for which Saussure used the English word *intercourse*. This centripetal-centrifugal opposition was of universal applicability, Saussure believed, relating not only to 'linguistic waves' and dialect variation but to *all* human customs. Indeed, when we consider some of the classic writings on 'groupness', this opposition does seem to possess broad significance. Distinctions have been drawn, for instance, between 'state and community', 'tribalism and globalism' and, of course, *Gemeinschaft* and *Gesellschaft*. All such distinctions reflect the tension inherent in desires to retain something valued – often something local, traditional or 'authentic' – in the face of larger, overarching and more impersonal forces. At the widest level, then, we are talking of matters of pluralism and assimilation, and with such tensions (as well, of course, as with the possibilities and aspirations with which they are associated), we can expect to see a wide variety of social and linguistic actions. At a simple level, for example, it is clear that linguistic practicality, communicative efficiency, social mobility and economic advancement have all become increasingly associated with large languages, thus interfering with the maintenance of smaller ones.

In many instances of language contact between varieties that are unequal in important ways, some bilingual accommodation seems to be the obvious avenue: one language for home and hearth, another for the world outside one's door. In many settings, however, bilingualism is often an unstable and impermanent way station on the road to a new monolingualism. There is, of course, *diglossia*, the more enduring state of bilingual or bi-dialectal coexistence. The complementarity here – whether of the classic sort, in which 'high' and 'low' forms of the same language co-exist, or in the broader sense that allows different languages to be the players – is stable almost by definition. But even stability is relative: nothing lasts forever, and diglossic arrangements need be no exception.

In settings involving powerful languages, and particularly in those where most 'mainstream' individuals are monolingual, stability is much harder to retain. Immigrant populations have always demonstrated this and, in those 'receiving' countries just mentioned, processes of language replacement are especially marked. Formal planning on behalf of languages that are or have become small can generally do very little to stem the forces of urbanization, modernization and mobility that place languages at risk. Decline in the existence and attractions of traditional lifestyles inexorably entails decline in languages associated with them. Short of unethical and draconian intervention, or of voluntary social segregation, language shift is often inevitable and bilingualism often a phenomenon that cannot be maintained beyond the second or third generation.

Despite the fact that some scholars write rather breathlessly about language 'loss', as if there were some period during which groups had no language at all, despite the fact that 'globalization' has become the longest four-letter word for many people, and despite the imbalance of heat and light in discussions of the social life of language, we should try to remember that change rather than stasis is the historical norm. Environments alter, people move and needs and demands evolve, and such factors have a large influence upon language. When considering accusations that certain societies, groups or institutions can be singled out as villains in the story of some language or another, we should keep some generalities in mind. Desires for social and economic mobility and advancement, and for the delights of modernity (however dubious) are, with some few notable exceptions, global phenomena. Whether we look at the capitalist world or the former communist one, at contemporary times or historical ones, at empires or small societies, at immigrant minorities or indigenous groups, we see a remarkable similarity of pressures and responses. Even when perceived to be generally positive, these are rarely without disadvantages or unwanted consequences. Change and transition often cause linguistic casualties.

It is not surprising that, because of its visibility and its overall position within culture, language is so often singled out for particular attention. Groups threatened with assimilation or unwanted integration by powerful neighbours, social and political activists, nationalists, cultural traditionalists – to say nothing of the many varieties of language enthusiasts currently found within and without academia – these are some of the constituencies for whom language retention, maintenance or revival becomes central. Since language, with its powerful symbolic value, is far more than merely an instrument of communication, it is entirely predictable that this pillar of group identity should assume special potency and centrality during times of uncertainty, anxiety and transition.

# Language Decline and Maintenance

Attempts to shore up a declining language are psychologically interesting even when the outcome is doubtful. In fact, language maintenance is often a parlous enterprise because, by the time a small variety is seen to require it, the precipitating social pressures have often assumed formidable proportions. It is also an enterprise that has typically been left to the amateur and the enthusiast. Quite commonly, it has been considered only a part of some broader literary revival. (In many such cases, concern for the oral or vernacular language has been much less pronounced than the interest in strengthening or, indeed, re-establishing some literary lineage.) I have already mentioned that linguists themselves have traditionally remained aloof from the fray, usually seeing in decline and shift a 'naturalness' that effectively precludes any useful intervention, even if that were thought desirable. Some contemporary scholars, however – generally sociolinguists, educators and sociologists, rather than linguists *per se* – have not shied away from engagement in the 'public life' of language. Joshua Fishman is a good example of one who is clearly committed to 'reversing language shift' among small languages, an undertaking he believes to be of spiritual significance. Fishman explicitly endorses a view of applied linguistics as *both* scholarship and advocacy, a stance shared by some others (see below), but one that perhaps involves some dangers.

There is a great deal of room for debate about this important matter, and about the appropriate postures for linguists and other concerned academics to adopt. I shall pay particular attention to 'language ecology' in the final chapter, but we can note here that the contemporary connection of language problems with broader 'green' issues – having to do with endangered species, threatened natural environments, atmospheric pollution, global warming and so on – has obvious political appeal, at least in the western world. It remains to be seen, however, just how appropriate such a connection is. One might suggest, for instance, that to speak of linguistic death and endangerment may be a variety of the pathetic fallacy; or, that it is considerably easier to save animals (given sufficient will, of course) than it is to rescue endangered languages; or, that such undertakings may suggest noble motives while, at the same time, revealing historical naïveté; or, that interventions on behalf of threatened languages reflect emotion rather than rationality. I will pick up some of these threads later on.

The languages and dialects most at risk have always been those that are both small and stateless, and their fate has become even more precarious in modern times. In a world in which the important lingua francas and the state-supported languages either ignored smaller and – it was presumed – unimportant media, or failed to penetrate their heartlands, the more localized forms continued on a minor but relatively stable basis. But that world has largely vanished. Now, the dominant languages are everywhere, and their intrusive power is ubiquitous. Their strength derives from the same political, social, military and cultural sources as always, but their scope has increased dramatically because of technological innovation on a scale never before seen. Their progress is like some juggernaut which crushes all in its path. Thus do English and

globalization (or westernization, or Americanization) march
arm-in-arm around the world.

There is another factor in all this, too. Apart from the
inexorable 'push' of a globalized economy, intent on selling the
same shoes, soft drinks and sex – through English – to everyone
from Boston to Bhutan, there is an almost equally powerful
'pull' factor. Globalization and its linguistic ramifications
are welcomed by many who see in it an upward mobility:
physical, social, psychological. All of this is very serious for
small languages without a state behind them, whose appeal to
their once-and-future speakers increasingly rests upon abstract
pillars of cultural continuity and tradition. The old English
proverb has it that 'fine words butter no parsnips': equally,
fine cultural appeals often seem empty to those to whom
they are chiefly addressed. I am not suggesting, of course,
some widespread revulsion at such appeals, or even ignorance
of them. The point, rather, is that bread-and-butter issues
continue to be the most important aspects of most people's
lives. Attention to more intangible matters tends to increase
as collars go from blue to white. Twenty years ago, Bernard
Spolsky wrote:

> A Navajo student of mine once put the problem quite
> starkly: if I have to choose, she said, between living in a
> hogan a mile from the nearest water where my son will
> grow up speaking Navajo, or moving to a house in the
> city with indoor plumbing where he will speak English
> with the neighbors, I'll pick English and a bathroom!

We may wish of course that families were not faced with such
dilemmas – that *Diné bizaad* could be spoken in a *hooghan*
outfitted with all mod cons – but this is not always possible.

Pressures also apply to languages that have state sponsorship,
but which are still small. One might imagine that a small language
with state support is powerfully armed, and such varieties do
indeed have increased chances of survival compared to their
stateless cousins, but it would be a great mistake to assume

that the acquisition of official status means that a corner has been decisively or irrevocably turned. Irish is the only Celtic language to have its own state, but that has not made it the most dominant in that family, nor has it proved possible to bar foreign linguistic influence at the customs-post.

A few years ago, I attended a meeting of the *Nederlandse Taalunie* (the Dutch Language Union) in Brussels. While its stated purpose was to examine the status and use of European languages, its real thrust was the place of the lesser-used 'national languages' – Dutch, Finnish, Swedish and so on – in a Europe increasingly dominated by French, German and, above all, English. About seventy participants from all over the continent (and beyond) provided more evidence than any rational observer could possibly need that being a 'state' variety rather than a 'stateless' one can mean very little in the world as it is today, and as it is likely to be in the foreseeable future.

If small varieties, with or without official political standing, are having difficulties, it seems obvious that these must be matched by favourable situations for large ones. A simple equation, however, that portrays the fate of the former as varying inversely with that of the latter is over-simplified. Of greatest importance here is the development of (at least) a two-category division in the ranks of the big languages. The first category has only one occupant (English), while the second comprises French, Spanish, German, Chinese, Arabic, Russian and other 'world' languages. There is considerable jostling for place in this second compartment, but less and less of it is felt in the neighbouring English basket.

Whether or not my very rough classification of languages and statuses is accepted, it is clear that intervention in them can be worse than doing nothing. Many language revivals have been put in train, many educational programmes have been devised to rejuvenate flagging varieties, and many community 'action plans' have been implemented (usually by outsiders). Few have had any noted success; many have been outright failures. A frequent stumbling-block has been inadequate preparation and inaccurate perceptions of local desires and needs. At a national level, the failure to bring Irish back as an ordinary vernacular is an example. At a local level, the failure of bilingual education programmes in the United States to prop up declining varieties – like French in New England, to cite a case with which I was very familiar – is another. A bigger stumbling-block has been the naïve assumption that scholars and researchers can do the work of statesmen and administrators. As the late Elie Kedourie astutely observed, intellectuals are not prime movers: academic research 'does not add a jot or a tittle to the capacity for ruling, and to pretend otherwise is to hide with equivocation what is a very clear matter'. For 'ruling' we could easily insert 'policy-making' or 'language planning'. And perhaps the biggest stumbling-block of all has been the myopic belief that languages exist in some independent form, such that work can be done on them in isolation from the larger social fabric.

To repeat what I wrote in the first chapter: language fortunes are *symptoms* of group interaction, and efforts directed towards language preservation alone are unlikely to have much substantial or durable success. It is only when thoroughgoing alterations in the social fabric have been made that we might expect to find significant and enduring linguistic change (among much else, of course). However, such widespread upheavals are rarely wanted by language and cultural revivalists. In the great majority of settings, the beneficiaries don't *want* to give up most of the other aspects of social life with which they have become familiar. It is doubtful, on both practical and theoretical grounds, whether the highly selective interventions desired by revivalists can hope to accomplish very much. It seems odd to think that serious scholars could actually believe that such picking-and-choosing were possible, but the academic literature testifies to the breadth of the mistaken idea that language intervention can be meaningfully conducted in some free-standing way.

I would not deny, of course, that scholars have real contributions to make in the social lives of languages, and the identities with which they are associated. But here are one or two points to consider. It would be useful, first of all, to cultivate a clearer and broader awareness of the *real* forces in the *real* world that bear upon language matters. To help reinforce the validity of language A, one can point to the internal 'logic' that all varieties possess, and rebut the incorrect view that some languages are inherently inferior to others. It may be useful to conduct studies showing the historical roots of language A, and to suggest that its continuity is bound up with that of its speakers' culture. It may be valuable to point to the imperialistic and basically unfair practices of those linguistic neighbours who are stifling the re-emergence of language A, or who are preventing it from maintaining its own little place in the sun. Such studies and concerns are, of course, eminently worthwhile from an academic and cultural point of view. If, however, we are concerned with *policy* and *planning* – and bearing in mind Kedourie's cautionary note – we should realize that none of this sort of work need have the slightest relevance to actual linguistic developments on the ground.

# Future Directions

The evolving relationships among small languages and large ones will certainly continue to be of central importance in the lives of many people. There are some particularly instructive contexts here. In the European Union, for instance, we see a continent coming together while simultaneously paying more attention to both 'stateless' and state languages of limited scope. Can an expanding federal Europe co-exist comfortably with a 'Europe of the Regions'? What is the status likely to be of languages like Danish and Finnish – to say nothing of Provençal, of Catalan, of Welsh? Of particular interest here, I think, is a deeper consideration of the technological 'shrinkage' of the world and its effects upon small varieties. On the one hand, for example, it can be argued that global technology assists the advance of English; on the other, that technology (together with European political restructuring) actually makes it easier for small cultures (and their languages) to have that desired place in the sun.

Relatedly, there will continue to be competition among the large languages. I have hinted already at what I consider to be the single most interesting question here: the emergence of a two-tiered structure within the ranks of the big languages. We need to know much more about the likelihood of English becoming super-dominant and the effects of this. This is important for the speakers of French, Russian and Spanish, but there are also obvious knock-on effects that will touch the smaller varieties. A world, or even a Europe, which evolves more and more to become 'English v Others' will not be the same as one in which the continuingly important presence of other large varieties interposes itself, as it were, between the super-language and the little ones.

Finally here, what about possible future developments in the use of a constructed language like Esperanto? In line with the points made a little earlier, I don't see that there is much more mileage to be gained in this direction – again, if we are interested in going beyond academically interesting pursuits and saying something about policy possibilities. There already exists a body of work outlining the internal structural regularity of Esperanto, the ease with it can be learned, the logic of having it as a universal second language that would not displace anyone's mother tongue, its desirably neutral status among a world of varieties burdened by particular histories and so on. But these things have to do with the language itself, and the really important matters (and they have always been central in the social lives of languages) have to do with sociological, political and psychological perceptions and prejudices. Why have constructed languages never really caught on? Even Esperanto, by far the strongest, has never managed more than a vestigial existence. Why are they so often seen (if seen at all) in negative or dismissive lights? What – realistically and practically – could possibly be done to increase their use? Isn't the case that, as universal lingua francas, their role has been more or less totally eclipsed by English? And so on. Within a reasonably large (but rather incestuous) literature, these sorts of questions have received much less attention than they ought to. Attempting to answer them would illuminate much more than constructed language alone.

It is vital to remember that what is really under discussion here is not so much group language as group *identity*. If language were purely an instrumental medium, then many elements of its social existence would resolve themselves, many of the most heated controversies and debates would vanish. Since language-as-symbol can be a key component of social-psychological 'groupness', however, the struggle between large and small varieties is often understandably vehement. We need always remind ourselves that this whole area is a heavily mined territory of emotion. Whatever the future may hold, this at least will be constant.

# CHAPTER NINE

# Endangered Languages and the Will to Survive

## What is Language Revival?

As I said in my opening remarks, language death may be an uncertain quantity but it is generally not difficult to identify languages whose health leaves something to be desired. The relative ease of making such identifications, however, hardly means that any ensuing interventions will also be easy. In fact, language maintenance and language revival are terribly difficult and complicated undertakings, and they rarely meet with much success. In part, this is because languages have usually become considerably constricted before any alarms are sounded. One consequence of this is that differences between 'maintenance' and 'revival' are often not nearly so pronounced as the terms themselves would imply. Besides, while 'revival' can certainly mean resuscitation, it can also, both logically and etymologically, refer to renewal, to reinvigoration, to the arresting of decline: to maintenance, in other words. Many forms or levels of restorative activity, then, can legitimately be placed under one heading of revival; the question is largely one of *degree* of difficulty and not of theoretical or principled difference. We could approach this from another direction and say that language maintenance shades into language revival: at all points along the continuum, a language is at some sort of risk. Such a continuum not only allows us to conceptually link two topics that are sometimes treated separately, it also returns us to the important matter of *gradation* – for, just as language death can be less than clear-cut, so can opinion vary about the likelihood and the success of language revival.

Osborn Bergin, a famous Irish philologist, once noted bluntly that 'no language has ever been revived, and no language ever will be revived'. A generation later, in 1953, Uriel Weinreich wrote that 'many "obsolescent" languages have received new leases on life'. A lot obviously depends upon one's assessments of language death and language revival. Furthermore, as contemporary scholars have pointed out, attempts to maintain and revive flagging languages may have beneficial consequences, even if they are ultimately and broadly judged as failures. Some commentators have felt, for instance, that the efforts to revive Irish have been unsuccessful, because the language never regained its lost vernacular status. Others have pointed out that compulsory Irish lessons at school have meant that a substantial minority of the population now claim at least a minimal command of the language (as we have seen). This may very rarely be put to any use, but it can at least be a base for further development for those who are interested. It can help to open a door to an ancient literature and mythology and to ancestral components of group identity. Entry here is severely hampered without at least a reading knowledge of the language. That being the case, can we say that the Irish revival has been a complete failure?

Different degrees and types of linguistic restoration can be put under the general rubric of 'revival' and, as I have just mentioned, determinations of success and failure are not necessarily clear-cut. This being so, we might give a little more attention to some specific matters. We might ask, for instance, if thoroughgoing revitalization efforts must always imply vernacular oral maintenance. Could a language preserved in written form, but spoken by few (or none) on a regular basis, be considered 'maintained'? The Irish experience might imply that the answer to this second question is yes: first, because the preservation of texts, and some ability to read them, can provide that doorway just mentioned; second, because such preservation could, at least theoretically, be a basis for future 're-vernacularization'.

In most instances, of course, we have to accept that language maintenance *is* meant to imply the continuity of some ordinary spoken medium. This, in turn, highlights the importance of uninterrupted domestic language transmission from one generation to the next. If this family transmission is sustained, then language maintenance is at some level assured; if, however, the passing of the linguistic torch from parents to children falters or ends, the language becomes very vulnerable indeed. Learning languages at the maternal knee has always been of the greatest importance in these matters. This is another way of saying that the home is probably the most important of all language *domains* – a point repeatedly, and correctly, stressed in the literature. Less often emphasized, however, is the logical ramification that, for the continuation of this domestic language setting, there must generally exist *extra*-domestic contexts within which the language is necessary or, at least, of considerable importance. Languages may most effortlessly and unselfconsciously be learned by small children at home, in that most private and intimate of settings, but the long-term prospects for them will still be dim if their usefulness disappears at the front gate.

And beyond that gate, we should remember that not all domains are of equal weight or value as pillars of language continuity. While it is difficult to be categorical here, it is possible to identify – for a given variety, at a given time, in a given context – what one might call *domains of necessity*. These domains are related to the most pivotal aspects of people's lives, and obvious examples include the home, the immediate community, the school and the workplace. On the other hand, domains in which participation is voluntary, or sporadic, or idiosyncratic, are not likely to be so important for broad language maintenance. The twice-a-week Welsh lesson may be intensely interesting, the teachers may be excellent, the materials and methods may be the newest and the finest, and the pupils may be strongly committed – but it is still a rather selfconscious world away from buying your groceries, routinely talking to your workmates, or having an after-dinner drink in the language. In summary, the maintenance of a language is on a surer footing if it, and it alone, is required in domains of central and continuing salience.

## Maintaining Domains of Necessity

Language maintenance is not, of course, an issue equally germane for all groups. It is, rather, one that assumes greater importance when a group and its language are at some risk of assimilation. For this reason, discussions of language minorities and language maintenance often coincide. I have already said that attention is typically given to a language only when it begins to lose ground (or is seen to be at risk of doing so), and that this complicates any attempts at maintenance or revival. Since small languages are typically associated with small communities, we can now see that linguistic difficulties are only one part of a much larger picture, a social and political picture in which many threats to group continuity may arise.

Although complicated in itself, and although made even more difficult by being only one thread in a broader and more all-inclusive social fabric, language maintenance *per se* can be quite easily problematized: how can a language be supported; how can decline and discontinuity be halted? There are two major and inter-related factors involved here, one tangible and one more subjective. The first I have already mentioned. It is the continuing existence of important domains within which the use of the language is necessary. These domains depend, of course, upon social, political and economic forces, both within and without the particular language community. Although the details will clearly vary from case to case, issues of general relevance include the linguistic practicality, communicative efficiency, social mobility and economic advancement that I touched upon in the previous chapter. These four constitute the greatest advantages associated with large languages, and the greatest disincentives for the maintenance of small ones. In many cases of language contact between varieties that are unequal in important ways, some bilingual accommodation is often sought but, as already suggested, bilingualism can be an unstable and impermanent phenomenon, one that will soon give way to a new monolingualism (in the stronger language).

Formal interventions, formal efforts at language planning on behalf of beleaguered languages and formal edicts from legislators can often do very little to stem the forces of urbanization and modernization which so often place languages in danger in the first place. (I am referring here, of course, to liberal-democratic contexts: dictatorial regimes have much greater powers of imposition, linguistic and otherwise.) Standardization and modernization are always theoretically possible, even for the 'smallest' of languages, but they are not always practicable, nor do they necessarily change in any substantial way the status-based balance of dominance among competing forms. Small varieties that have developed to national-language levels (Somali in Africa, and Guaraní in South America, for example) still remain less broadly useful than English and Spanish, respectively. In fact, their usefulness drops off quite dramatically as soon as one leaves their heartlands.

As I have already noted once or twice – but the point bears much repeating – language decline and shift are typically *symptoms* of contact between groups of unequal political and economic power. They are effects of a larger cause. Just as one does not cure measles by covering up the spots, so one cannot maintain a language by dealing with language alone. To switch metaphors and perspectives: large-scale social changes meant to float all boats would certainly float linguistic ones, but such alterations are generally not desired. Even the most fervent linguistic and cultural nationalists are unlikely to want such wholesale flooding. The hopes are narrower, revealing a wish for a linguistic rejuvenation coincident with the uninterrupted continuation of other desirable aspects of current social life. Many of the latter reflect the benefits afforded by participation in (or next to) the large community whose incursions have brought about language decline in the first place. You see the problem?

# Willingness

The more intangible or subjective factor in language mainte- nance and revival efforts, and certainly the more interesting from a psychological viewpoint, is the matter of the collec- tive *will* to stem discontinuity. The objection is sometimes made that, since language decline is often a reflection of rela- tive social inequality, it is unrealistic to expect that threatened cultures and sub-cultures can exercise much power or actu- alize their desires. In general terms, this is true, and the evi- dence is all around us. There are, however, some subtleties here that are worth exploring, some nuances that a broad-brush perspective may not capture. In their studies of the decline of the Celtic languages, scholars have charted the familiar terri- tory of linguistic retreat in the face of the advance of English. But they have also pointed out that acquiescence in at least some facets of language shift (notably in educational settings) coincided with strong resistance to other manifestations of 'mainstream' pressure: the parents who were apparently will- ing enough for their children to be educated through English were at the same time quite capable of violent protest over land-management matters. The Highland Scots (for example) increasingly came to associate English with three life-altering phenomena. Two of these were employment and prosperity, while the third – emigration – demonstrates the awareness that material advancement comes at a cost.

The Celtic varieties, however, came to acquire quite different connotations. One researcher suggested that these smaller languages gradually became associated with 'childhood, song and dance'. In fact, this is a little too simplistic: it paints only a lightly regretful picture of an immature, if pleasant, past which must be left behind. The reality, for both indigenous and immigrant minority groups, usually involves rather stronger links and a rather more poignant balance sheet of plusses and minuses. Nonetheless, choices are made and linguistic associations naturally reflect them. If we stay with the Celtic languages for another moment, we find that early nineteenth-century Irish became more and more linked with 'penury, drudgery and backwardness'. Self-perceptions of Gaelic in Nova Scotia were described in almost exactly the same words by another commentator: the language implied 'toil, hardship and scarcity'. English, by contrast, was a medium of 'refinement and culture'. From the time of the earliest emigrations, settlers in the new world 'carried with them the idea that education was coincident with a knowledge of English'. It goes without saying that I am making no judgement here about the accuracy or, indeed, the desirability of such attitudes. I only wish to point out that perceptions of languages and, therefore, the desires and actions that rest upon them are based upon comparative assessments and that, as resistance in other quarters indicates, there is some evidence for a reasoned discrimination here, even in subject populations.

The sufficiency of will required for the assumption and exercise of power has, historically, been more evident in some areas than in others; recall here that Scottish resistance to land 'reform', to the 'clearances'. Groups whose clout is evident in economic areas (think of the increasing commercial and political accommodations made for Spanish speakers in the United States today) may not be as apparently demanding in others. Why not? Why do people who go to the barricades for some things seem to acquiesce in others – in matters of language shift, for example? There is, of course, simple inertia, an inherent problem wherever passivity is to be galvanized into action. There are clear reasons for this, most of them having to do with lack of sufficient awareness coupled with the economic and pragmatic imperatives that affect ordinary life; these touch everyone, of course, but rather more centrally for those who are of subordinate or disadvantaged status. So, it often proves difficult or impossible to translate a rather inert goodwill into something more dynamic. (Language revival efforts, for instance, are typically characterized by a small group of activists nervously glancing over their shoulders to see how many of their presumed adherents are following them.)

It is also possible for populations to have been 'taken in' by mainstream groups, so that they no longer know or trust their own linguistic and cultural instincts. Drawing upon earlier work showing how negative, authoritarian and prejudiced evaluations of stigmatized social and religious groups were sometimes replicated *within* these groups themselves, social-psychological researchers in Montreal described a 'minority-group reaction' by which small linguistic communities may come to believe that their language is indeed deficient vis-à-vis that of the larger surrounding population.

While these sorts of explanations imply a group inadequacy that action in other arenas makes unlikely (think once more of those struggles over land, but also remember resistance to religious and legal impositions), it is undoubtedly the case that, as Desmond Fennell wrote, 'the lack of will to stop shrinking is an intrinsic characteristic of a shrinking language community'. An acquired frailty of will is perhaps a more general manifestation of the Montreal findings; it is certainly a deeper and more subtle manifestation than any superficial listlessness and, even if it is only restricted to some areas of psychosocial life, it presents a gritty problem. It reflects, in fact, powerful factors already touched here, notably the contact between unequal groups, communities or systems, and the socioeconomic changes set in train by this contact.

If will is a quantity that can be galvanized in some circumstances, how important is it? At a recent language symposium in Germany, Joshua Fishman argued that it was an imprecise concept, and that examples of its explanatory power were hard to delineate (a very curious stance for him to adopt: see below). In fact, however, there are cases that seem very obvious indeed. After enduring long years of socio-political and religious paternalism, the francophone population in Quebec experienced a *révolution tranquille*, transformed and modernized itself, and assumed the provincial mastery that its inherent strength had always promised. An important corollary of the transformation was linguistic engineering on behalf of a French language considered to be at risk. Thus, Bernard Spolsky writes of francophones beginning to become 'conscious of English dominance'; he uses terms like 'commitment' and 'ideological support', states bluntly that 'language policy is about choice' and emphasizes the importance of the 'perception' of sociolinguistic situations. These usages are not all (or always) synonymous with will, but they all suggest how important convictions, attitudes and perceptions are in matters of language maintenance and revival.

Other more immediately relevant examples also suggest themselves. At that German conference, for instance, Fishman gave a plenary address, part of which consisted of a list of many intangible aspects of sociological and linguistic power, and virtually all of these could just as easily have been described in terms of the operation of will. More pointedly, he made reference to the decision in his own family to create and maintain a Yiddish-speaking home. This is quite clearly an illustration of conscious will power at work, of a decision taken on the grounds of conviction rather than practical necessity. It is also a personal reflection of the broader argument about the importance of family transmission of languages from one generation to the next that I have already mentioned. If one family can make certain language choices, then others might do so as well. We could recall here the far-reaching effects of Eliezer Ben-Yehuda's creation, in the 1880s, of the first Hebrew-speaking home in what was to become Israel; his son, born in 1882, was the first maternally Hebrew-speaking child in the modern era. To be able to extrapolate, then, from the family to the community would be of the greatest importance in the life of 'threatened' varieties.

In fact, Fishman has made many references to will in his writings. He has observed, for instance, that the success of the re-vernacularization of Hebrew rested upon 'the rare and largely fortuitous co-occurrence of language-and-nationality ideology, disciplined collective will, and sufficient social dislocation'. In discussing efforts on behalf of Frisian, he wrote that 'the basic problem seems to be in activating this [passive] goodwill'.

The invocation of the concept of will is surely also accurate when we consider the actions of those strongly committed to the protection of at-risk languages. Language nationalists, activists and enthusiasts are typically few in number but fiercely committed to their linguistic cause. Consider the Cornish and Manx revivalists, or those native anglophones who move to the *Gaeltachtaí* of Ireland and Scotland, or those who carry the banners for Gaelic in Cape Breton Island, and so on; there are many apposite cases here. The other side of this coin – and the one that often gives the activities of revivalists their poignancy – must obviously be the will of those who choose *not* to move to minority-speaking enclaves, or to bring up their children in some threatened medium, or to otherwise encourage it. It might be thought that this second category is not particularly interesting or illuminating, representing merely passivity, *non*-exercise of will, or a decision to not make a decision, to drift along in the current of some mainstream. In fact, however, there are contexts in which conscious decisions unfavourable to minority languages, on the part of potentially important players, are equally illustrative of the power of active will.

It is a testament to the depth and sensitivity of the German symposium to which I have already twice referred that one of the most important of these contexts, the post-colonial setting, was extensively discussed, notably by Africans and Africanists. It was frequently pointed out, for example, that one consequence of colonialism is that the élites in newly-independent countries have typically been educated abroad; their training is usually undertaken in the language of the former colonizers and they often continue to value that language more highly than indigenous varieties. When it comes, then, to encouraging local vernaculars and their development, or opting for the mediums of education, the mindset of those in power is (or so it is alleged) still stuck in a linguistic rut. The operation of *their* will stifles local languages, even perhaps their own mother tongues. Given the great divides that often exist between the rulers and the ruled, the implication is that a change in that mindset, a recalibration of that will, could have profound consequences for those large numbers who are linguistically and educationally excluded from the corridors of power, whose languages remain widely used but unfairly reined in. It is, of course, of the greatest significance that the exercisers of will in these circumstances are indigenous individuals themselves: they may be the élite, socioeconomically far removed from the vast majority of their compatriots, but they are unquestionably *of* the place. They are not callous outsiders whose language policies, however reprehensible, are understandable in the traditional colonial context. Rather, they are people of whom more might have been expected. Indeed, they are people who often *have* fulfilled the expectations of them in other matters of social and political life.

The poignancy of all this has been eloquently discussed in a number of essays by the distinguished Kenyan author (and now faculty member at New York University), Ngũgĩ wa Thiong'o. His decision to write in Gĩkũyũ and not in English is an important part of the backdrop to his many impassioned pleas for the linguistic and cultural 'decolonizing' of the African mind, and to his indictment of those in power whose minds apparently remained colonized. In one essay, Ngũgĩ wa Thiong'o cited an observation by another famous writer, Chinua Achebe:

> Is it right that a man should abandon his mother tongue for someone else's? It looks like dreadful betrayal and produces a guilty feeling. But for me there is no other choice. I have been given the language and I intend to use it.

Achebe surely speaks here for many 'third-world' intellectuals but, for Ngũgĩ wa Thiong'o, Achebe's position is morally untenable. The former bluntly notes that 'African literature can only be written in African languages' (he does not accept the argument, by the way, that European varieties have *become* African languages through adoption). He is particularly concerned with literary and dramatic 'decolonization', but he has certainly commented upon politics as well. He writes about Léopold Senghor, for instance, who admitted that French had been forced upon him but who yet remained 'lyrical in his subservience' to the language; and about Hastings Banda, who created an élite English-language academy in Malawi, staffed by teachers from Britain, and expressly designed to encourage able students to be sent to universities in England and America.

To summarize: the importance of linguistic and cultural *will* and its ramifications can hardly be denied. The importance rests, ultimately, upon matters of *perception*, the demonstration of whose centrality to social life is the single greatest insight of modern psychology. Matters of perception are not necessarily matters of fact: we are dealing here with intangibles, but what is intangible is often the strongest and the most resistant to change, or to cultural adversity or endangerment. As Ernest Renan observed, more than a century ago, 'une nation est une âme, un principe spirituel' in which the single most important factor is the group will. In fact, he contrasted this explicitly with language: 'il y a dans l'homme quelque chose de supérieur à la langue; c'est la volonté.'

# CHAPTER TEN

# Linguistic Intervention and the 'New' Ecology of Language

## Scholarship and the Social Life of Language

Given the formidable attractions associated with large languages and their host societies, it is not surprising that *active* moves for language maintenance are typically found among a relatively small number of people. There are, of course, practical reasons why the masses (particularly in subaltern societies) find it difficult to involve themselves in maintenance efforts, even if they are generally sympathetic – their collective *will* must often remain of a broad but passive nature. To animate this rather inert quantity has always been the most pressing issue for language activists. Many years ago, in commenting upon the efforts to sustain Irish, David Moran made a point that is still relevant in many quarters: 'without scholars [the revival] cannot succeed; with scholars as leaders it is bound to fail'.

As we have seen, linguists and other language scholars have traditionally considered most cases of language decline and shift to be part of a more or less natural process, part of very broad historical patterns. Thus, in my earlier discussion of purism and prescriptivism, I noted that intervention has typically been seen as neither desirable nor feasible. I also pointed out, however, that some contemporary scholars have not shied away from engagement in what might be called the 'public life' of language, and some have argued that a combination of scholarship and advocacy is reasonable and desirable. Joshua Fishman, for instance, has suggested that a deeply felt regret over mother-tongue loss provided the catalyst that brought many researchers into linguistics and related fields in the first place. He has certainly made no secret of his own commitment and has devoted considerable attention to the question of 'reversing language shift', an undertaking that he deems a 'quest' of 'sanctity'.

Fishman's contribution to the revival literature lies in the addition of dispassionate argument to a strong personal commitment to the cause of 'threatened' languages. But, as in the writings of other revivalists of one stripe or another, the lines of demarcation between scholarship and involvement can easily become blurred. For example, just as Douglas Hyde, the famous Irish revivalist and statesman, equated anglicization with a hated modernity, so there are elements in Fishman's work that suggest that language revival is associated with the desire to reawaken earlier and (allegedly) better values. He has written of the reversal of language shift as an important factor in the battle against the banalities of modern life, against 'market hype and fad'. He has expressed concern about a contemporary 'peripheralization of the family' and the current disregard of 'moral and spiritual dimensions'. Such sentiments illustrate a common thread in the writings of language activists: they wish to take radical steps on behalf of conservative impulses. The implication seems to be that, once linguistic and cultural wrongs have been rectified, once the depredations of large and powerful neighbours have been halted, there will be a return to some 'smaller' and purer time. And yet, for all this, activists are loath to admit any orientation to the past. Indeed, Fishman writes that 'there is no turning the clock back'. Nonetheless, phrases like those I have just quoted do rather suggest that he might – after all – be glad to see the clock run back a bit, and that his most basic sympathies lie with some mythical 'better' or 'smaller-is-beautiful' past. This sense is reinforced when we find him describing the reversal of shift as also 'reversing the tenor, the focus, the qualitative emphases of daily informal life' or, more bluntly still, as 'remaking social reality'.

When Fishman describes advocates of language shift reversal as 'change-agents on behalf of persistence', he provides a perfect illustration of what I have just referred to as radical action in the service of conservative ideals. It would be unfair to single Fishman out here, by the way: the sentiments he expresses, and the hopes he entertains, are common to all language nationalists. In fact, one of the pillars of nationalism itself is the selective mining of history in the construction and preservation of group identity. Here is Renan again: 'l'essence d'une nation est que tous les individus aient beaucoup de choses en commun, et aussi que tous aient oublié bien des choses'. All nationalists look to the past in order that, suitably manipulated, it can be made to serve their current needs and aspirations.

A few years ago, the pages of the American journal, *Language*, provided a discussion in which matters of scholarship and advocacy figured centrally. Michael Krauss pointed with alarm to the large number of the world's languages now in danger; more than half are now moribund, he argued, and few are likely to survive to the end of this century. Setting the tone for much of the debate that was to follow, he said that linguists will be 'cursed by future generations' if they do not actively intervene to stem the 'catastrophic destruction' now threatening nine out of ten of the world's languages. Traditional emphases on varieties of linguistic documentation are insufficient, according to this interpretation. Social and political action and advocacy are required. Linguists must go well beyond the usual academic role of description and documentation, Krauss argued, 'promote language development in the necessary domains ... [and] learn ... the techniques of organization, monitoring and lobbying, publicity, and activism.'

Peter Ladefoged responded by saying, in effect, that personal preferences ought not to become intertwined with scholarly activity, reinforcing the traditional view that it is not the duty of researchers to try and persuade groups that language shift is a bad thing (or, of course, a good thing). He reminded readers that not all speakers of threatened varieties see their preservation as either possible or desirable, and his general position was that an intellectual perspective, too, should not necessarily look upon language shift as 'catastrophic destruction'. Ladefoged went on to observe that

> one can be a responsible linguist and yet regard the loss of a particular language, or even a whole group of languages, as far from a 'catastrophic destruction' ... statements such as 'just as the extinction of any animal species diminishes our world, so does the extinction of any language' are appeals to our emotions, not to our reason.

A third participant in this exchange was Nancy Dorian, who noted that all arguments about endangered languages are political in nature, that the low status of many at-risk varieties leads naturally to a weakened will-to-maintenance, that the loss of any language is a serious matter, and that the laying out of the 'facts' advocated by Ladefoged is not a straightforward affair, since they are inevitably intertwined with political positions. At the very least, Dorian noted, this is an 'issue on which linguists' advocacy positions are worth hearing.'

We have, in fact, come to hear more and more about the positions taken by scholars and researchers. Apart from a number of excellent anthologies dealing with endangered varieties, there also exist several organizations devoted to the preservation of diversity, to the 'ecological' perspective, to active intervention on behalf of threatened languages. They include the Endangered Language Fund, the Committee on Endangered Languages, and Terralingua (all based in the United States), Linguapax (in Barcelona, affiliated with the Endangered Language Fund), the Foundation for Endangered Languages (in England), Germany's *Gesellschaft für bedrohte Sprachen*, and the International Clearing House for Endangered Languages (Japan). Similar concerns have motivated the European programmes of Linguasphere and the *Observatoire linguistique*, as well as those groups and individuals whose more pointed purpose is language-rights legislation.

It is clear that this is a very contentious area. What some would see as inappropriate and unscholarly intervention, others would consider absolutely necessary. Any combination of scholarship and advocacy is fraught with potential danger, but one might reasonably argue that one of the 'facts' to be presented to groups and policy-makers is the very commitment of at least some in the academic constituency. Groups whose languages are at risk might profit from the knowledge that the issues so central to them are also seen as important by outsiders, and that the problems they are facing are not unique. At the end of the day, though, we should remember that, whether fervently pro-maintenance in tenor or more 'detached', the actions of linguists are likely to pale when compared with the realities of social and political pressures. Such realities should at least suggest a sense of perspective.

# The 'New' Ecology of Language

This is precisely where the contemporary and 'new' ecological awareness stakes its claim: it purports to offer fresh ways of understanding this social tissue of influence and, by implication, new approaches to linguistic maintenance and revival. These typically involve bilingual solutions, in that a continuing bilingualism is generally seen as the most reasonable accommodation for small or 'at-risk' varieties. This is not unreasonable, since the alternative – some monolingual emphasis upon the threatened variety alone – is an increasingly unlikely (and unpopular) course of action. While we have already seen that bilingual or diglossic stability is neither easily achieved nor effortlessly maintained, attention to it is hardly misplaced.

I suggest, however, that the novelty of much of the current green ecological thinking is chimerical. Einar Haugen, the linguist who popularized the ecological metaphor for language matters, clearly noted that the concept was a reworking of older models. After all, the essential idea – that language matters are political and social, and must be considered in their contexts – has long been accepted. The breadth that might reasonably be expected in a field of study now calling itself the 'ecology of language' is also more apparent than real (which, as we shall see, is why I write about it in the particular context of endangered varieties). While the ecological insights of the nineteenth century were concerned with adaptations of all kinds, with the Darwinian 'web of life' and the famous struggle for existence, and with relationships ranging from the beneficial to the brutal, contemporary views have downplayed competition and have emphasised coexistence and coöperation. Thus, Peter Mühlhäusler has written that

> functioning ecologies are nowadays characterized
> by predominantly mutually beneficial links and only
> to a small degree by competitive relationships ...
> metaphors of struggle of life and survival of the fittest
> should be replaced by the appreciation of natural kinds
> and their ability to coexist and cooperate.

This is an inappropriate and unwarranted limitation. More reasonable is the earlier and more fully Darwinian observation of William Mackey: linguistic environments (like all others) can be 'friendly, hostile or indifferent'. In the new ecology, however, we are given a view of a world in which there is room for all languages, where the goodness of diversity is a given, where 'the wolf also shall dwell with the lamb'. This is certainly a kinder and gentler picture, but the key word in Mühlhäusler's quotation is 'should', and the key question is whether the desire is also the reality. We might remember Woody Allen's reworking of that passage from Isaiah: 'the lion and the calf shall lie down together, but the calf won't get much sleep'.

The new ecological thrust is driven, above all, by the desire to preserve linguistic diversity in a world where more and more languages are seen to be at risk, and where matters of maintenance and revival are central. Attempts have been made to link this thrust with current environmental concerns for biological diversity, protection of wildlife and so on. This linkage is understandable and perhaps useful at a metaphoric level. In a world where opinion can be activated to save the whales, preserve wetlands, rescue rare snails and owls or, indeed, to keep historic buildings from the wrecker's ball and to preserve and restore rare books and paintings, why should we not also try to stem language decline and prevent linguistic predation? It is interesting (but not, perhaps, surprising) that, in some quarters, the linkage has been seen as *more* than metaphoric, with the suggestion that linguistic and biological diversities are co-extensive, mutually supportive, possibly even 'co-evolved' (as Luisa Maffi put it). The most basic problem with such an organic approach to language is, of course, that language is not organic. Languages themselves obey no natural imperatives, they have no intrinsic qualities that bear upon any sort of linguistic survival of the fittest, they possess no 'inner principle of life'. The implication is clear: attempts to go beyond a purely metaphorical relationship between linguistic and biological diversity will soon find themselves on dangerous ground, ground that biological amateurs would do well to avoid.

There are one or two other revealing aspects of the new ecolinguistics that I must touch upon here. It is commonly assumed, for instance, that human 'interference' has created the necessity for ecological management and planning; healthy ecologies, we are told, are both 'self-organizing' and 'self-perpetuating', but human action often upsets the balance. This is, of course, a naïve and inaccurate stance: in what sphere of life have human actions *not* altered things? Indeed, what social spheres could there possibly be *without* such actions? This seems like lamenting the fact that we have two ears. We also note here the curiously static quality of much ecology-of-language thinking. The implication often seems to be that – once some balance is achieved, some wrong righted, some redress made – the new arrangements will, because of their improved moral basis, be self-perpetuating. But history is the graveyard of cultures, not all of which have been unremittingly pleasant, incidentally.

The new ecology of language is also critical of literacy and education, on the grounds that they often undercut the preservation of linguistic diversity. Indeed, it is sometimes argued that literacy promotion actually works against the vitality of small languages. Literacy is seen as a bully: written varieties push oral ones aside, writing is more sophisticated than speech; and so on. It would surely be a dangerous instance of isolationism, however, to try and purchase language maintenance at the expense of literacy. A related suggestion is that formal education is not always the ally of enduring diversity and bilingualism, for it often has intrusive qualities, championing literacy over orality, and imposing foreign (i.e. western) values and methods upon small cultures. Again there is the idea of cultural bullying. It is not difficult to sympathize with laments about supposedly intrusive 'foreign' education paradigms but, since *all* education worthy of the name is multicultural in nature, the argument is self-defeating. Formal education necessarily involves broadening the horizons, going beyond what is purely local and 'traditional'. In an unequal world, whose disparities create risks for languages, education will perforce become yet another evidence of those disparities.

Any discussion of the 'moral' foundations of the new ecology quickly brings up the matter of 'linguistic human rights'. Ecological organizations formed expressly for the protection of endangered languages typically have a charter or a statement of intent stressing these curious entities. The Teachers of English to Speakers of Other Languages organization (TESOL) passed a resolution in 2001, for example, asserting that 'all groups of peoples have the right to maintain their native language … a right to retain and use [it]'. The other side of the coin, they argue, is that 'the governments and the people of all countries have a special obligation to affirm, respect and support the retention, enhancement and use of indigenous and immigrant heritage languages'.

There are many problems associated with language rights. Official and quasi-official resolutions and charters, for example, are often outlined in a manner so general as to be virtually useless, or are written without any accompanying intent to act. And there are deeper issues, too. Language rights are usually meant to have an effect at the group level; indeed, their existence is generally motivated by the plight of small groups whose languages and cultures are at risk. This may sit uneasily with traditional liberal-democratic principles that enshrine rights in individuals, not collectivities. This is not the place for fuller discussion, but it should be noted that wider matters of pluralist accommodation in societies that are both democratic and heterogeneous, where language rights are obviously a subset of concern, are now of the greatest importance. They have become part of the province of political philosophy, for instance, which implies a very welcome breadth of approach, a search for cross-society generalities, an escape from narrower and intellectually unsatisfying perspectives. The discussions here, whatever their specifics, and however their strengths and weaknesses may be perceived in different quarters, all suggest that any isolated statement or claim of language rights is simplistic and unprofitable.

There are even more basic issues with which the framers of language-rights manifestos rarely engage: do rights even exist and, if they do, what sorts of things are they? Perhaps there are no rights; perhaps there are only cultural claims. Rights to language seem not to be of the same order as, say, those that proclaim freedom from slavery. While legal rights imply moral ones, the reverse does not necessarily hold (although what is merely desirable today may of course become lawfully codified tomorrow). The difficulty for moral claims is to effect this transition. For now, at least, this has generally not occurred, and it is disingenuous to imply that *claims* are sufficient to somehow give language rights the same strength of footing as those rights underpinned by criminal or civil codes. And there is, above all else perhaps, a powerful practical matter to be faced here. While it is possible to legislate rights of language expression, it is rather more difficult to legislate rights to be *understood*; typically, this has occurred only in very limited domains (in selected dealings with civil services, for example), not in the vast unofficial ones where languages really rise or fall. And if your language is not understood by people with whom you must deal, its usefulness is rather restricted.

Many current perspectives on language diversity and its inherent 'rightness' suggest a rejuvenation of more general, romanticized nationalistic assertions. Thus, models of the new ecology of language tend to identify some types of political villains more readily than others: unrestrained free-market capitalism, unfettered industrialization and galloping globalization all come in for heavy criticism. And, just as eighteenth-century romanticism was a reaction to more enlightened thought, so it has again become possible to find disparagement of the scientific culture and concern for the 'privileging' of its knowledge over 'folk wisdom'. There is a special regard for small cultures and local knowledge, and it takes two forms: first, a simple, straightforward and, indeed, perfectly reasonable desire for the survival of such cultures and systems; second, the argument that they are in some ways superior to larger societies and values. This view is generally expressed in some muted fashion, but occasionally the mask slips: some lines of dedication in a recent anthology were directed 'to the world's indigenous and traditional peoples, who hold the key to the inextricable link between [sic] language, knowledge and the environment'.

Overall, the 'new' ecology of language is not so much a refinement of scientific methodology in the face of new understandings and new challenges as it is a sociopolitical ideology. It is interesting that an ecology that, by its nature, ought to be multi-faceted, inclusive and, above all, aware of nuanced perspectives, should often see things in rather simplistic ways. My critical remarks here are not directed at ecology *per se*, of course, for who could gainsay its essential elements? But I think that the underlying ideology of the new ecology of language is insufficiently examined and, in fact, builds in various assumptions as if they were unremarkable, and beyond enlightened debate. While some of its underpinnings may be appropriate in some cases, there can be little doubt that a wholesale acceptance of them would be both unwise and counterproductive.

Endangered languages, and the identities with which they are associated, are of obvious interest to linguists, and some of the latter now seem more or less committed advocates in the service of language maintenance, most centrally via the new ecology of language. The area is now very much a growth industry, but it is hard to see that it has done anyone any good – except, of course, for those scholars who have found ample opportunity for publishing arguments on the side of the angels, and for fostering debate, if only among themselves. While the latter development is a common one across all sorts of scholarly discourse, there is surely a special poignancy here, inasmuch as virtually all the writing is presumably meant to have applied value, intended to make a real contribution to the lives of those whose small languages and cultures are overshadowed by large and overbearing ones. While it is an acknowledged duty of intellectuals to avoid oversimplification, search out explanatory nuance and probe with scholarly lancets rather than the blunter instruments wielded in less sophisticated or disinterested quarters, I am tempted to say that a great deal of the research effort here has been misguided, disingenuous or both.

The narrow focus of most modern writing on linguistic ecology is upon an environmentalism that makes a specific case for the maintenance of diversity. This is not problematic in itself, of course, and it is clearly not an illegitimate stance (although it is not always a sturdy one), but it is surely reasonable to have some misgivings about an area that describes itself in very broad terms while, at the same time, marshalling its forces along quite specific lines. My central criticism is that language maintenance and revival are always difficult endeavours, that past efforts have often foundered on the shoals of romantic and unrealistic enthusiasm and that approaching the topic from a position of aesthetic and moral commitment, while understandable and in some circumstances even laudable, is neither in the best traditions of disinterested scholarship nor likely to realize long-term success.

A preference for diversity, linguistic and otherwise, is one that I share; indeed, I find it difficult to imagine that any educated perspective would vote for monotony over colour, for sameness over variety. But to see the new ecology as largely undergirded by this preference is not only to criticize its rather more grandiose assertions, it is also to suggest that the old difficulties in maintaining endangered languages have not, after all, been lessened through new insights. These difficulties have, indeed, been heightened and exacerbated in modern times, as more and more languages and language domains fall under the shadow of English. How might endangered languages best be supported? One would certainly be more indulgent towards the formal shortcomings of the 'new' ecology if its assumptions and its programmes actually seemed to make a difference on the ground. In fact, however, these shortcomings only serve to highlight difficulties that have been quite well understood for some time. Most of these can be summarized by observing (yet again) that, unless one is interested only in some archival embalming, the maintenance of languages involves much more than language alone. To put it another way, the conditions under which a variety begins to suffer typically involve a stronger linguistic neighbour and, hence, language endangerment is symptomatic of deeper matters, a particular sort of fall-out from a larger collision. Acknowledgement of this simple and indisputable statement of affairs must surely suggest the scope of the difficulties commonly encountered.

# EPILOGUE

As implied in the prologue, my treatment here of what could be termed the 'social life of language' is, at some sub-surface level ( not a *very* deep one, however), not really about language at all. Or, rather, it is about language as a particular window into the human condition, language as a perspective from which to consider social interaction, language as a marker of individual and group definition. The unique approach afforded by studying language rests upon two important facts. The first of these is simply that language is ubiquitous: there has never been a human group without language – well, not for a very long time anyway – and every language is adequate for the immediate needs of its speakers. A corollary here is that language is eminently mutable: as circumstances and requirements alter, language will adapt and develop.

The second important fact is that language is almost always more than an instrumental or communicative medium. Stripped-down technical vocabularies, pidgin varieties and constructed languages are the obvious exceptions here, exceptions arising from quite specific and essentially prosaic needs. But, as I have noted, even these spartan communication devices will, if circumstances are propitious, begin to add further layers of meaning and nuance. Technical lexicons can merge into common parlance and, themselves, take on metaphorical meanings far beyond their restricted origins. (Computer terminology provides a good case in point, with terms like *download* and *interface*. I recently read, too, of the use of *hardware* and *software* to refer to the brain and its thought contents, respectively. And a computer colleague informed me that dull people can be described as having *ROM* – read-only memory, that is, incapable of taking in new information.) Pidgin varieties, as we have seen, can become creolized as they migrate towards the status of 'natural' languages. And constructed forms like Esperanto begin to show regional variation; as well, with the development of original written material, particularly poetry, they too take on more nuanced and non-instrumental aspects.

The single most important message that I have tried to convey in this book is that all discussions of the social life of language are ultimately discussions about group identity. The very diversity of languages, discussed in the opening chapters, is a testament to the desire to maintain particular and unique windows on the world. Purely instrumental mediums would, over the long haul of history, have shown much greater tendencies to converge than natural languages have done, and visitors to the Earth from outer space might find it odd that a species so adept in many other ways seems so backward in taking the obvious steps to facilitate wider and easier global communication. In Chapters 5 and 6, I turned to some of the obvious consequences of a multilingual world and, with particular regard to translation, we saw again how the imperatives of 'groupness' can intertwine with the clear necessities of cross-border communication, or, to put it another way, how the symbolic aspects of language coexist with more mundane and instrumental ones. The interesting phenomenon of 'voice appropriation' is a particularly poignant example of the importance of language as it bears the weight of social narrative and group myth.

The final chapters consider the same language-and-identity relationship in the highly-charged contexts of language contact and conflict. If the symbolic value of language is important, then it is entirely understandable that societies finding themselves in states of transition – most centrally when these have been forced upon them by external pressures, but even where transition is generally welcomed or self-initiated – will be particularly sensitive to questions of language maintenance and shift. And more than that: in many settings, it is to be expected that groups will act to keep their languages 'pure', that they will fight to preserve varieties seen to be threatened by powerful linguistic neighbours, and that possibilities for formal intervention on behalf of flagging varieties will be considered more closely.

My aim here has been to present succinctly some of the important constituents of language-in-society settings, some of the factors that must be attended to in any meaningful discussion. I have also hoped to provide a treatment that can be read by people at all levels of linguistic sophistication: is there *anyone* who isn't interested in the social life of language at some level or other? Finally, I hope I've suggested – implicitly throughout much of the book, rather more explicitly in one or two places – that we need clearer and more dispassionate perspectives. In areas that often generate more heat than light, in contexts in which scholars often become advocates, in settings where virtually everyone has strong opinions – in such circumstances, this need is surely magnified.

# NOTES AND REFERENCES

## Prologue

The remarks of President Clinton that I have paraphrased here were made in his capacity as keynote speaker at the official opening of the Frank McKenna Centre for Leadership, St Francis Xavier University, on 11 May 2011. McKenna, currently the Chairman of the University Board of Governors, is a former premier of New Brunswick (1987–1997) and Canadian Ambassador to the United States (2005–2006).

## Chapter 1: The Diversity of Languages

The observations about 'first languages' draw upon my new book, *Inventing Languages* (in preparation). The citation from Joachim du Bellay is on pp. 46–47 of his *Defence and Illustration of the French Language*, first published in 1549 (London: Dent, 1939). The quotation by Edward Sapir is in his *Language* (New York: Harcourt, Brace, 1921, pp. 19 and 222). Useful general treatments of New Guinea include John Waiko's *Short History of Papua New Guinea* (Melbourne: Oxford University Press, 1993), *A Short History of New Guinea*, by Peter Biskup *et al.* (Sydney: Angus & Robertson, 1970), and Laura Zimmer-Tamakoshi's *Modern Papua New Guinea* (Kirksville, Missouri: Truman State University Press, 1998). For the observation by

Sir William 'Oriental' Jones, see Frederick Bodmer, *The Loom of Language* (London: Allen & Unwin, 1943, p. 180). The quotations about the scope of English are from David Crystal's *English as a Global Language* (Cambridge University Press, 2003, 2nd edition, pp. 69 and 189). One of the classic works linking genetics and linguistics is *Gènes, peuples et langues*, by Luca Cavalli-Sforza (Paris: Jacob, 1996).

# Chapter 2: Interpreting Language Diversity

For the case of Marie Smith Jones, and Eyak, see Mary Pemberton, 'Last of the Eyak' (*Globe & Mail* [Toronto], 25 January 2008) and the obituary in *The Economist* (9 February 2008). An interesting twist on the 'last-speakers' phenomenon came to light very recently, when *The Guardian* (13 April 2011) noted that only two fluent speakers of Ayapaneco, a Mexican language, now remain. However, Manuel Segovia and Isidro Velazquez refuse to talk to one another, even though they live just 500 metres apart. A curiosity in itself, to be sure, but perhaps also a reminder of the internal divisions that so often occur within small communities – often at the very time, outsiders frequently observe, when some sort of Dunkirk spirit might be expected, and would certainly be useful. In *Globalization and Language Vitality* (London: Continuum, 2008), Cécile Vigouroux and Salikoko Mufwene present many examples of the complexities of influence among languages in contact.

Miss Blimber appears, of course, in Chapter 11 of *Dombey and Son* (first published serially by Charles Dickens, beginning in 1846). The classic discussion of group boundaries vis-à-vis the cultural content enclosed within them remains Fredrik Barth's *Ethnic Groups and Boundaries* (London: Allen & Unwin, 1969). For the discussion of Latin, see Gael Branchereau, 'Blue suede sandals' (*Globe & Mail* [Toronto], 18 August 2007) and Tommasso Mariucci, *Latinitas nova et vetera* (Vatican City: Libreria Editrice Vaticana, 1986–1991, 5 volumes).

The analysis of Bhadranna Mallikarjun, of the Central Institute of Indian Languages, is very useful, and it is from his 'Language according to Census of India 2001' (see http://www.languageinindia.com/april2001/indiancensus.html) that I have drawn the two quotations.

On group names, see George Stewart's *Names on the Globe* (New York: Oxford University Press, 1975). The famous 'army and navy' quotation is by Max Weinreich, see the discussion in my *Language and Identity* (Cambridge University Press, 2009). The quotation about Serbo-Croatian is found on p. 84 of Ranko Bugarski's important discussion, 'Language, nationalism and war in Yugoslavia' (*International Journal of the Sociology of Language*, 2001, 151, 69–87); see also Robert Greenberg's *Language and Identity in the Balkans: Serbo-Croatian and its Disintegration* (Oxford University Press, 2004).

# Chapter 3: Multilingual Abilities

On bilingual and multilingual abilities, see my 'Forlorn hope?' (in Li Wei, Jean-Marc Dewaele and Alex Housen [eds], *Opportunities and Challenges of Bilingualism*. Berlin: Mouton de Gruyter, 2002) and 'The importance of being bilingual' (in Jean-Marc Dewaele, Alex Housen and Li Wei [eds], *Bilingualism: Beyond Basic Principles*. Clevedon: Multilingual Matters, 2003). The Spanish-English code-switching citation can be found in David Crystal's *Cambridge Encyclopedia of Language* (Cambridge University Press, 1987, p. 363). The quotation by Voltaire is reproduced by John Waterman, *A History of the German Language* (Seattle: University of Washington Press, 1966, p. 138). For the remarks by Carew, Rivarol *et al.* – and, a little later on, those by Bacon, Butler and Milton – see my *Challenges in the Social Life of Language* (Basingstoke: Palgrave Macmillan, 2011) and the earlier *Multilingualism* (London: Penguin, 1995).

The quotation from 'my' teacher is on p. 339 of a study published with Margaret McKinnon, 'The continuing appeal of disadvantage as deficit' (*Canadian Journal of Education*,

1987, 12, 330–349). The other teacher's remark is from Rosina Lippi-Green's *English with an Accent* (London: Routledge, 1997, p. 111).

For the quote from William Mackey, see his article, 'The importation of bilingual education models' (in James Alatis [ed.], *Georgetown University Round Table on Languages and Linguistics*. Georgetown University Press, 1978, p. 7).

James Murray's letter is cited by Katherine Murray, *Caught in the Web of Words* (New Haven: Yale University Press, 1977, p. 70). The remarks about Sir Richard Burton draw upon Dane Kennedy's book, *The Highly Civilized Man* (Cambridge, Massachusetts: Harvard University Press, 2005). My reference to Paulin Djité's multilingual fluencies is substantiated in his own recent book: *The Sociolinguistics of Development in Africa* (Clevedon: Multilingual Matters, 2008). George Steiner discusses his trilingualism in his *After Babel: Aspects of Language and Translation* (Oxford University Press, 1975).

There is a large literature on bilingual education and its ramifications; see Colin Baker, *Foundations of Bilingual Education and Bilingualism* (Bristol: Multilingual Matters, 2011, 5th edition); see also my more general *Language Diversity in the Classroom* (Bristol: Multilingual Matters, 2010).

On 'superdiversity', transnationalism and the quotation about assimilation, see p. 551 in Angela Creese and Adrian Blackledge, 'Towards a sociolinguistics of superdiversity' (*Zeitschrift für Erziehungswissenschaft*, 2010, 13, 549–572); and these same authors for the references to discursive practices (on p. 555), 'playfulness and creativity' (p. 565), 'we are obliged ...' (p. 554), social inequities and reinvention (p. 554), 'plurality of affiliation' (p. 568) and 'the ability to language ...' (p. 570). Their references to inequities and reinvention are taken from Sinfree Makoni and Alastair Pennycook's 'Disinventing and reconstituting languages', a chapter in their edited collection of the same title (Clevedon: Multilingual Matters, 2007); and that to 'the ability to language' from Ofelia García's 'Languaging and ethnifying' (in Joshua Fishman and Ofelia García [eds], *Handbook of Language and Ethnicity*. Oxford University Press, 2010).

'What exactly is wrong …' is found on p. 337 of Stephen May's 'Language rights' (*Journal of Sociolinguistics*, 2005, 9, 319–347). On 'translanguaging', see Ofelia García's foreword to the Makoni and Pennycook collection, noted above; her quotation ('an arrangement …') is found on p. xiii of this foreword, and is citing the work of Colin Baker, 'Biliteracy and transliteracy in Wales' (in Nancy Hornberger [ed.], *Continua of Biliteracy*. Clevedon: Multilingual Matters, 2003); her note about 'mixed language practices', in which she cites Makoni and Pennycook, is also on p. xiii.

García is also the author of the citation about 'more inclusive of differences', which appears on p. 387 of her *Bilingual Education in the Twenty-First Century* (Oxford: Wiley-Blackwell, 2009).

The citations about 'translingual language practices …' and 'separable and enumerable categories' are from 'Disinventing and reconstituting languages', the chapter by Makoni and Pennycook (pp. 36 and 2), noted above.

Mikhail Bakhtin's famous essay, 'Discourse in the novel' is now most easily found in *The Dialogic Imagination* (Austin: University of Texas Press, 1981); it first appeared in 1934.

# Chapter 4: The Emergence and Measurement of Multilingualism

Arthur Koestler's description of Jewish linguistic variation can be found in his controversial book, *The Thirteenth Tribe* (London: Picador, 1980, p. 157). For fuller details on the technicalities of censuses, see my edited volume, *Language in Canada* (Cambridge University Press, 1998), the earlier *Multilingualism* (Penguin, 1995), and the article 'Canada/Kanada', which appeared in the third volume of *Sociolinguistics/Soziolinguistik*, edited by Ulrich Ammon, Norbert Dittmar, Klaus Mattheier and Peter Trudgill (Berlin: Mouton de Gruyter, 2006). Lionel Wee's very recent paper, 'Language policy mistakes in Singapore' (*International Journal of Applied Linguistics*, 2011, 21, 202–221) discusses a rare governmental admission of flawed language policies.

# Chapter 5: The Consequences of Babel: Lingua Francas

John Dryden's reference to 'lingua franca' appears in his play, *The Kind Keeper, or, Mr. Limberham* (London: Bentley & Magnes, 1680). The 'aesthetic' dialect studies were conducted in the 1970s by Howard Giles and his colleagues; see my *Language and Identity* (Cambridge University Press, 2009).

The citation from Julius Berncastle is on p. 65 of the second volume of his *Voyage to China* (London: Shoberl, 1850). That from Peter Trudgill is on p. 170 of his *Sociolinguistics* (London: Penguin, 2000, 4th edition). Andrew Dalby's *Dictionary of Languages* (New York: Columbia University Press, 1998) provided the Krio examples (on p. 331).

For the section on constructed languages, I have drawn again on my *Inventing Languages* (in preparation). See also Roberto Pellerey, *Le lingue perfette nel secolo dell'utopia* (Rome: Laterza, 1992); Umberto Eco provided a preface to this work before producing his own *Ricerca della lingua perfetta nella cultura europea* (Rome: Laterza, 1993).

Zamenhof's observation is reproduced on p. 96 of E. J. Lieberman, 'Esperanto and trans-national identity' (*International Journal of the Sociology of Language*, 1979, 20, 89–107), who also provides the note about 'facts, texts ...' (p. 100). And Orwell's blunt remark appeared in his 'As I please' series for *Tribune* (28 January 1944).

# Chapter 6: The Consequences of Babel: Translation

George Steiner's several observations are from his *After Babel: Aspects of Language and Translation* (Oxford University Press,

1975, pp. 233, 250, 251 and 285), in which the quotations from Talleyrand, Ortega y Gasset, Popper and (a little further on) Dryden will also be found (pp. 46, 224, 225 and 256). Wittgenstein's note is in his *Tractatus Logico-Philosophicus* (London: Routledge & Kegan Paul, 1974, p. 114).

My discussion of 'voice appropriation' draws upon my *Language and Identity* (Cambridge University Press, 2009). Leonard Tancock's remarks are in the prefaces to Émile Zola's *L'Assommoir* (Harmondsworth: Penguin, 1970, pp. 16 and 18) and *Germinal* (Penguin, 1954, p. 16). The reference to Émile Rieu is found in the latter preface. Vladimir Nabokov's observation is on the first page of the foreword to his translation of Pushkin's *Eugene Onegin* (New York: Pantheon, 1964). See Josef Škvorecký's 'Literary murder at five cents a word' (*English Today*, 1985, 4, 39–42) for further reference to Nabokov, and to Dreiser, Dickinson and Christie; the direct quotations are on p. 40.

# Chapter 7: Keeping Languages Pure

George Thomas's important study is *Linguistic Purism* (London: Longman, 1991). Maurice Druon's remarks were made under the title 'Le franc-parler: non-assistance à langue en danger' (*Le Figaro*, 24 February 2004). On popular views of language decline and decay, see Randolph Quirk's *Style and Communication in the English Language* (London: Arnold, 1982); the direct citations from his book are on pp. 99 and 59. George Orwell's 'Politics and the English language' appeared in *Horizon* (April 1946). Dwight Bolinger's remarks are found in his *Language: The Loaded Weapon* (London: Longman, 1990). Bill Mackey's observation is found on p. 55 of his 'Language diversity, language policy and the sovereign state' (*History of European Ideas*, 1991, 13, 51–61). See also my *Language and Identity* (Cambridge University Press, 2009) for the observations by Verstegan, Defoe and Swift; the *Restitution of Decayed Intelligence* (London: Norton & Bill, 1605); and my *Inventing Languages* (in preparation).

The 2010 *Economist* piece, 'This time we mean it', can be most easily consulted at www.economist.com/blogs/johnson/2010/06/english_academy. The website of the Queen's English Society is www.queens-english-society.com.

Samuel Johnson's *Plan of a Dictionary* was published in 1747 (London: Knapton *et al.*), followed by the famous dictionary itself (in 1755); the direct quotations are from the (unpaginated) preface to the latter.

On American developments, John Adams, etc., see Shirley Heath, 'A national language academy? Debate in the new nation' (*International Journal of the Sociology of Language*, 1977, 11, 9–43); see also Glendon Drake, *The Role of Prescriptivism in American Linguistics, 1820–1970* (Amsterdam: Benjamins, 1977). Noah Webster's dictionary was published in New York, by Converse, in 1827; the direct citation is from his *Grammatical Institutes* (Hartford: Hudson & Goodwin, 1783, p. 7).

# Chapter 8: Languages and Identities in Transition

Saussure's ideas are documented in the *Cours de linguistique générale*, edited by Charles Bally and Albert Sechehaye (Paris: Payot, 1980). On language decline and maintenance, see Joshua Fishman, *Reversing Language Shift* (Clevedon: Multilingual Matters, 1991). For further general information, see my 'Language and the future' (in Humphrey Tonkin and Timothy Reagan [eds], *Language in the Twenty-First Century*. Amsterdam: Benjamins, 2003); and *Language, Society and Identity* (Oxford: Blackwell, 1985).

Spolsky's citation is found on the last page of his review of Colin Baker's *Key Issues in Bilingualism and Bilingual Education* (*Applied Linguistics*, 1989, 10, 449–451). Elie Kedourie's remark is found in his *Nationalism* (London: Hutchinson, 1960, p. 125).

# Chapter 9: Endangered Languages and the Will to Survive

There are many excellent treatments of 'at-risk' languages, including *Endangered Languages*, edited by Lenore Grenoble and Lindsay Whaley (Cambridge University Press, 1998) and *New Perspectives on Endangered Languages*, edited by José Flores Farfán and Fernando Ramallo (Amsterdam: Benjamins, 2010). See also my *Language and Identity* (Cambridge University Press, 2009), *Minority Languages and Group Identity* (Amsterdam: Benjamins, 2010) and *Challenges in the Social Life of Language* (Basingstoke: Palgrave Macmillan, 2011).

Osborn Bergin's observation is cited by Tomás Ó hAilín on p. 91 of 'Irish revival movements' (in Brian Ó Cuív [ed.], *A View of the Irish Language*. Dublin: Government Stationery Office, 1969, p. 91). Uriel Weinreich's is found in his *Languages in Contact* (The Hague: Mouton, 1974, p. 108). The comments about Irish, Gaelic (in Nova Scotia) and English are those of Caoimhín Ó Danachair, 'The Gaeltacht' (in the Ó Cuív anthology, p. 120); Charles Dunn, *Highland Settler* (University of Toronto Press, 1974, p. 134); and John Campbell, 'Scottish Gaelic in Canada' (*An Gaidheal*, 1948, 43, 69–71).

See Wallace Lambert *et al.*, 'Evaluational responses to spoken languages' (*Journal of Abnormal and Social Psychology*, 1960, 60, 44–51) and *Attitudes and Motivation in Second-Language Learning*, by Robert Gardner and Wallace Lambert (Rowley, Massachusetts: Newbury House, 1972) for the Montreal work on the 'minority-group reaction'.

For the observation about the lack of will to resist 'shrinking', see p. 30 in Desmond Fennell's 'Can a shrinking linguistic minority be saved?' (in Einar Haugen, Derrick McClure and Derick Thomson [eds], *Minority Languages Today*. Edinburgh University Press, 1981).

Discussion of the German language symposium, including the remarks cited by Joshua Fishman and Bernard Spolsky, can be found in my chapter, 'The power of language, the language of power' (in Martin Pütz, Joshua Fishman and JoAnne Neff-van Aertselaer [eds], *Along the Routes to Power: Explorations of Empowerment Through Language*. Berlin: Mouton de Gruyter, 2006). For the direct quotations from Fishman, see his *Reversing Language Shift* (Clevedon: Multilingual Matters, 1991, pp. 291 and 180). Chinua Achebe's remarks are cited by Ngũgĩ wa Thiong'o in his *Decolonising the Mind: The Politics of Language in African Literature* (London: Currey, 1986, p. 7). The latter's own remarks are found on pp. 19 and 27.

The famous observations by Ernest Renan can be found in Henriette Psichari's edition of the *Oeuvres complètes de Ernest Renan* (Paris: Calmann-Lévy, 1947, pp. 899 and 903).

# Chapter 10: Linguistic Intervention and the 'New' Ecology of Language

David Moran's point was expressed in his essay, 'The Gaelic revival' (*New Ireland Review*, 1900, 12, 257–272). Fishman's remarks are from his *Reversing Language Shift* (Clevedon: Multilingual Matters, 1991), and full details can be found in 'What can (or should) linguists do in the face of language decline?', my contribution to *Papers from the Seventeenth Annual Meeting of the Atlantic Provinces Linguistic Association*, edited by Margaret Harry (Halifax: Saint Mary's University, 1994).

Renan's note about selective memory is in Henriette Psichari, *Oeuvres complètes de Ernest Renan* (Paris: Calmann-Lévy, 1947, p. 892).

The discussion involving Michael Krauss, 'The world's languages in crisis' (*Language*, 1992, 68, 4–10); Peter Ladefoged, 'Another view of endangered languages' (in the same volume, pp. 809–11); and Nancy Dorian, 'A response to Ladefoged's other view of endangered languages' (*Language*, 1993, 69, 575–79) – with the direct citations from Ladefoged and Dorian on p. 810 and p. 579, respectively – is treated in my 1994 chapter (cited above).

On the 'new' ecology, see my chapter, 'The ecology of language: insight and illusion' (in Angela Creese, Peter Martin and Nancy Hornberger [eds], *Ecology of Language*. New York: Springer, 2008). The quotation about 'mutually beneficial links' is on p. 308 of Peter Mühlhäusler's 'Language planning and language ecology' (*Current Issues in Language Planning*, 2000, 1, 306–367). William Mackey's remark is from 'The ecology of language shift' (in Peter Nelde [ed.], *Languages in Contact and Conflict*. Wiesbaden: Steiner, 1980, p. 35).

The note about 'co-evolution' is on p. 175 of Luisa Maffi's 'Language preservation vs. language maintenance and revitalization' (*International Journal of the Sociology of Language*, 2000, 142, 175–190). A note in my *Challenges in the Social Life of Language* (Basingstoke: Palgrave Macmillan, 2011) touches upon somewhat more sophisticated approaches to relationships between language and the natural world; see Chapter 6, note 7. The remarks about 'interference', and so on, are found on p. 310 of Mühlhäusler's article.

The TESOL resolution appears in *TESOL Board of Directors Reaffirms Position on Language Rights* (Alexandria, Virginia: TESOL, 2001). The quotation citing indigenous peoples' special environmental knowledge is in Luisa Maffi's dedication to her edited collection, *On Biocultural Diversity* (Washington: Smithsonian Institute Press, 2001). For fuller discussion of language rights, see also my 'Contextualizing language rights' (*Journal of Human Rights*, 2003, 2, 551–571).

# INDEX

Although there is some overlap, this index generally omits entries for material that is easily found under a heading or sub-heading shown in the table of contents.